THE WORK
OF OUR HANDS

THE WORK
OF OUR HANDS

Jewish Needlecraft for Today

Mae Shafter Rockland

SCHOCKEN BOOKS • NEW YORK

Photographs by Elaine Miller, Miramar Photo, and Barbara Russo

TO THE GENERATIONS:

*My grandparents, David and Raisel,
Yehudah and Chaya Faigle, who lived
in the villages of the pale of
settlement and still live in my
imagination;*

*My parents, Joe and Bella Shafter, who
have imparted to me their great love
for the people Israel;*

*My husband, Michael, Song of Songs
5:10–16;*

*Our children, David, Jeffrey, and Keren
Chaya, inheritance from the eternal.*

Preface

DURING AND AFTER the years of World War II, when I was growing up in the East Bronx in New York City, I did a lot of sewing—mostly rag dolls and their clothes. My mother would often look at me with her head to one side and say: "If your *bobe* [grandmother] was only here, she would help you. She would sew you anything you want. She had *goldene hent* [*golden hands*]." And I would dream about that *bobe*. Somehow she had escaped from Poland and was trudging bloody up the hill from the subway, and I would recognize her and run to greet her, and bring her to our warm apartment where, after some recuperation, she and I would sit and sew—she the teacher, I the adoring and adored disciple.

Of course, she never came; she is, as my mother says, "with all the other Jews." But the fantasy persisted for a long time. All I have of her are some photographs and needlework. One of the photographs was taken before World War I and shows her as a young matron, sitting proudly wearing her *sheytl* [wig] and a long black dress, my mother at three in ruffles beside her. Another, taken in 1923, also with my mother and her older brother, my uncle. This time she wears no wig —it is after the Russian Revolution, and the three of them are wearing high-necked Russian jerseys. They stare earnestly into the camera; this is the photograph by which they are to remember each other, because my mother and uncle, at sixteen and eighteen, are to go to America to try for a better life.

I look at these photographs, and at the three pieces of needlework my mother brought with her to America, and I continue to fantasize. I never start a sewing project without talking it over with my *bobe* first.

I discussed this book with her too, and, as you will see, each section of it is introduced by a personal note or historical material or both. I trust the reader will find my occasional nostalgic passages illustrative rather than self-indulgent. Although the book is basically a work manual for the sewer, I hope the nonsewer will enjoy browsing in it as well.

I have attempted to offer needlework projects that can be accomplished by following designs similar to dressmaking patterns. It is hoped that this approach will encourage individual expression in the reader–sewer while at the same time offering enough structure to help her overcome initial fears of working without a kit. It is hoped, too, that this will be a step toward creative participation in a Jewish-American Folk Art movement.

What is currently available in crafts for Jewish-Americans, either to buy or to make, is paltry indeed. If we go looking for a *matzah* or *hallah* cover to buy, we find that the only objects available are far below even Green Stamp standards. In the Jewish Museum in New York City there are a few well-designed objects available for purchase, but these few are hardly representative of the size, vigor, and affluence of the American Jewish community. Certainly many fine things are available from Israel, but American Jews should not be solely dependent on our Israeli brothers and sisters to produce all of our Jewish objects. If we are truly interested in enriching our aesthetic and religious lives simultaneously, we shall have to make the things ourselves.

This is a time when American Jews are searching for ways to express and define their Judaism. At the same time, American women, in spite of (or because of) labor-saving devices, are turning more and more to the crafts as a way of expressing their individuality. Amateur art groups are springing up all over the country. Painting, ceramics, découpage, embroidery, weaving, batik, jewelry-making, leathercraft, and carpentry groups are finding work for hands left idle by a mechanized age. It seems natural to combine both of these longings—to make things and to enrich our Jewish lives—and to turn them in a historically and culturally significant direction. Psalm 90 says it all:

> Let Thy work appear unto Thy servants,
> And Thy glory upon their children.
> And let the graciousness of the Lord our God
>   be upon us;
> Establish Thou also upon us the work of our
>   hands;
> Yea, the work of our hands establish Thou it.

Tishri 5733 / September 1972

Acknowledgments

THIS BOOK IS the product of many conversations with good friends. Sandie Rabinowitz, Ruth Schulman, and Marcia Sternberg, of the Princeton, New Jersey, Chapter of Hadassah, encouraged the project in its early stages. Rabbi Hershel J. Matt provided both scholarly and spiritual guidance. Trudy Glucksberg was instrumental with her editorial and artistic advice, as well as her moral support. Margaret Bolton, Linda Goodman, and Aviva Pinchuck gave generously of their time by providing me with a sounding board and by reading early drafts. Michael Rockland gave me the benefit of his historical insights and literary skills. Beverly Colman, my editor at Schocken Books, spurred me on with her enthusiasm and expertise.

With few exceptions, the projects shown here were designed especially for this book. They were fully worked out and tested, as I wanted to make sure that, in all cases, I was giving you the "recipe" that would work in your "kitchen." If I had had to do it alone, the needlework in this book would have taken years to realize; but I was very fortunate to have excellent friends and students who lent their talents for the making of many of the projects. Without them, this book could never have come to be. My most heartfelt thanks and appreciation to Nancy Amick, Joyce Becker, Sheva Bernstein, Jacqueline Brown, Maxine Farmer, Jane Kahn, Natalia Morgan, Keren Rockland, Marion Roemer, Cecelia Rosenblum, Emma Spence, Sylvia Schwartz, Shirley Watson, and Frances Zeitler. There were times when I felt as if I were running a sweatshop. But now we can all, finally, just relax and have a cup of coffee.

Contents

PART TWO: THE PROJECTS

Contents   xiii

ONE

THE BASICS

An Approach
to Jewish Art

IT IS CONVENTIONALLY believed that Jews have never distinguished themselves in the plastic arts. Most art-history books do not discuss the Jews at all when they deal with the "great civilizations" of the ancient world. Even apologists consider the words "Jewish" and "art" as somehow antithetical and immediately cite the Second Commandment, which they interpret as a prohibition against artistic endeavor, when, in reality, it was meant to discourage idolatry, not art.*

Those who depend heavily on the Second Commandment as "proof" that the Jews have no art are limiting the definition of art to that which is representational. Most of the world's art is nonrepresentational. Also, the endless concern with the "Jewish art question" has had an inhibiting effect, not so much on the production of works of art as on the recognition that a body of Jewish art exists and indeed has always existed.

From their earliest wanderings in the desert, the Jews have been concerned with creating beautiful material forms for their demanding religion. In the very barrenness of the desert, God told Moses to construct an elaborate tent of worship and pointed out to him that among the slaves who had come out of Egypt was a master craftsman, Bezalel, who was familiar

* "Thou shalt not make unto thee a graven image, nor any manner of likeness, of any thing that is in heaven above, or that is in the earth beneath, or that is in the water under the earth; thou shalt not bow down unto them, nor serve them" (Exodus 20:4–5).

with all the techniques of metalwork, weaving, embroidery, and carpentry needed to create the beautiful sanctuary desired by God (Exodus 31:35–36).

It is true that Jews have rarely had the kind of security, wealth, and power that are essential to the production of immense art works and edifices. In the Jewish tradition, the primary function of wealth has always been to feed the needy, to help the widow, orphan, and poor scholar, rather than to construct luxurious edifices and monuments. But this does not mean that no art existed—just that much less of it was created in costly silver, gold, and marble. Artistic expression found its outlet in the less precious and, unfortunately, more perishable wood, brass, paper, and clay. But we should value the materials no less: the material does not make the artist. A work of art grows from the sensibility that the artist brings to the materials. Works executed in these humbler materials often have great emotional power because they relate directly to life, without any intervening "intrinsic value."

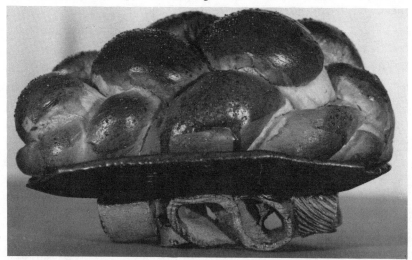

FIGURE 1: Recently "bread sculpture" has become very fashionable. For centuries, Jewish women have created special breads for the Sabbath and festivals. The traditional braid is shown here, placed on a contemporary dish I made for the Sabbath. The complex base imitates the curves of the *hallah*

Before the intellectual and political emancipation of Jews in the last century, Jewish artistic expression consisted primarily of synagogue decoration, calligraphy, and the creation of ritual objects. While synagogues have never equalled church art in majesty and opulence, the different purposes of each must be considered. The synagogue is meant to serve as a meeting and study house as well as a house of prayer, while the church is meant as a setting for the dramatic enactment of the Miracle of the Mass.

Much of Jewish religious observance takes place at home, around the family table. The historian Cecil Roth has commented that "Jewish [family] life gained in warmth what the synagogue lost in artistic beauty." * Throughout the ages, folk artisans have made *menorot*, candlesticks, Sabbath lamps, wineglasses, *hallah* covers, spice boxes, and Passover articles to enhance the many observances in the life cycle of the Jewish family. Wealthier people would commission things in precious metals from professional silversmiths; and often, since through much of the Middle Ages in Europe the Jews were largely excluded from the guilds, articles of gold and silver were made by Christian artists. In Moslem lands, on the other hand, most metalwork was left in the hands of Jews and other non-Moslems, so that many Moslem art objects were created by Jewish artisans.**

Since the emancipation, and especially since the advent of abstract art, the numerically small Jewish people has contributed many notable artists to the world.

Some may argue that unless a particular artist's work deals

* *Jewish Art: An Illustrated History* (Tel Aviv, 1961; New York and London, 1971).

** Even in Europe by the end of the Middle Ages Jewish craftsmen sometimes produced work for Christian religious use. In the New World, where Jews were at last free to choose their own occupations, the first President of the New York Gold and Silver Smiths' Society was the Revolutionary War veteran Myer Myers, who produced many beautiful ritual objects, among them *rimmonim* [Torah rod finials] for the Touro Synagogue in Newport, R.I. (now a national shrine), as well as a great deal of secular ware.

with recognizable Jewish subject matter or symbols, the work of that artist cannot be considered "Jewish." The problem of "What constitutes Jewish art?" is as thorny as the problem of "Who is a Jew?" I would define Jewish art liberally: as any artwork that was created by someone of Jewish origin, that was made for a Jewish function, or that incorporates Jewish values or themes in its design. I am aware that this definition may not be acceptable to everyone, but I find it a workable one for me. Therefore, for me, the early work of Ben Shahn is Jewish art, as is his later work which is more specifically Jewish in theme. At the same time, Modigliani's work is part of Jewish art. Furthermore, since, as I mentioned earlier, much of Jewish ceremonial art was produced by Christian artisans, I would certainly include the magnificent synagogues produced by Frank Lloyd Wright and Minoru Yamasaki as Jewish buildings and, therefore, as forming a part of the Jewish artistic tradition.

Objects and symbols

In Israel today, archaeology is the national hobby. One after another, legendary sites and figures have become realities as their physical remains have been uncovered.

The Bar Kokhba caves revealed not only letters by this leader of the Second Revolt against the Romans (132–35 C.E.) but utensils and textiles used by his followers. These objects graphically show us that, even in the unbelievably difficult conditions of life in a cave high above the Dead Sea, the followers of Bar Kokhba observed Jewish law and custom. Never was there any evidence of the mixing of different fibers —those of linen with those of wool—which is forbidden by Mosaic law; the ritual fringes were removed from the garments used as shrouds; and other ritual fringes [*tzitzit*] in progress were found. The nineteen vessels unearthed were of obvious Roman manufacture, adorned as they had been with figures of pagan deities. Jews of this period were extremely icono-clastic, risking torture and death to remove the Roman eagle from public places, so it was with great interest that Professor Yadin noted that the images on these utensils used in the privacy of a cave were defaced by filing: sometimes the entire image was obliterated, sometimes just enough of the nose was abraded away to make it acceptable for use by those ultra-orthodox freedom fighters.*

Centuries from now, when archaeologists are digging up our remains, what artifacts will they find to indicate that the Jews who lived in twentieth-century America lived by Jewish values? While we accumulate Jewish book and record collections, we often tend to dismiss the possibility of making our visual surroundings identifiably Jewish in aesthetic terms. Part of the reason for this may be that too much of what has recently been called Jewish art has consisted of depictions of mournfulness masquerading as spirituality. Beloved as he may be, the praying, bearded rabbi is not the only subject matter available to Jewish art. Throughout the difficult periods of Jewish history, there have always been the glimmer of hope for a better world and an uncanny ability to make the most of what we have in this world.

As we live we either create or destroy. Every act should be an affirmation, an Amen to the Creation. We clutter our lives with unnecessary products and ornaments, the excreta of American affluence. How many of these things reflect our inner values? With a little effort and study, we can enrich our own lives and those of our children by giving additional meaning to our visual surroundings.

Articles for holiday or ritual use are Jewish by their very nature. Whether or not they have inscriptions on them, they

* Yigael Yadin, *Bar-Kokhba: The Rediscovery of the Legendary Hero of the Last Jewish Revolt against Imperial Rome* (Jerusalem, London, and New York, 1971).

are identified by their use. A wine goblet becomes a *kiddush* cup, a special napkin a *hallah* cover; any plate can be used as a Seder plate. Making the ordinary, secular objects of daily life "look Jewish" is more difficult and, therefore, challenging. Every act has profound overtones. If we want to make a Jewish object, we should ask ourselves what the Jewish philosophical approach to the action, symbolized by the article, is and try to imbue what we are making with this philosophy or feeling.

One source of decoration is to find appropriate Hebrew quotations (considering our vast literature, this is not very difficult) and use attractive letters to write them on the object you are making. Care must be taken in the choice of inscriptions. If quotations and slogans are going to be used, they should serve a greater function than simple identification. Just as writing BREAD on a breadbox doesn't necessarily make it a more satisfactory breadbox, writing לחם [*lehem*] will not necessarily make it a more Jewish breadbox.

An object is made Jewish by the function it performs, by an appropriate inscription, or by the use of Jewish symbols in its decoration. The Jew, forever mindful of the pitfall of idolatry, has always had an ambiguous relationship to realistic representation. He has allowed his artistic gifts freer rein in symbolic and abstract expression. I would love to be able to give you a list of authenticated, 100% Jewish symbols, but many symbols were common property throughout the Middle East and were adopted by the Jews (e.g., the Tree of Life). Others have changed hands so frequently that, although they may have a long Jewish pedigree, we hesitate to claim them—(the fish, dove, winged angel, cherub). Still others, such as the *magen David*, though very new as Jewish symbols, are used so commonly that they are in danger of becoming clichés.

Symbols are powerful abstractions of basic human activities such as eating, fighting, and sex, which are all interrelated. The largest category is sex, fertility symbols dominating all others. As nomadic shepherds and then agricultural people, the Jews lived close to the seasons and to the earth. Biblical metaphors and symbols point directly to life-giving forces and preoccupation with fertility. The tenacity and longevity of Judaism are owed to the adaptability and incorporation into abstract thought of these most basic, primitive human feelings and concerns. So often we find that symbols remain the same, but interpretations of them have completely changed. The transformation of the Tree of Life from a multifruited fertility symbol to a symbol of the Torah as the nourisher of mankind is such a case. Symbols once used in rain and fertility rites (the *lulav* [palm branch] and pillars) have become invested with emotions of dedication, redemption, and messianic hope. It is difficult from such a historical distance to know how long the ancient meaning lived on inside the shells of their respective symbols. Material and spiritual needs merge in these ancient symbols. Jewish faith was centered on a monotheistic concept of an invisible God. When something more tangible was needed, the Hebrews found it in symbols that offered reassuring group identity while pointing to a higher abstract truth. In the contemporary world, symbols that were once the center of religious worship persist as part of our cumulative culture and, though stripped of venerative meaning, live on as emblems of our common fate. This intense group identity has in turn infused profound meaning into yet other symbols.

When will the swastika cease to make us shudder? For tens of centuries this symbol existed as a sign of perpetual motion, of fertility, of the sun. It had many and various meanings in different cultures at different times in history. Some say it originated with the Hebrews as a sign for the flaming swords of the cherubim that guarded the entrance to the Garden of Eden after Adam and Eve were turned out (Genesis 3:24). Will the swastika ever regain its earlier meanings or will it be indelibly engraved in the mind of man as the symbol of evil and brute force?

The simple double triangle, the *magen David*, called the Shield of David or Jewish Star, has within it the power to invoke intense emotional response. It is popularly considered to be *the* symbol of Judaism, in the same way that the cross symbolizes Christianity, and the crescent, Mohammedanism. Yet this six-pointed star, though an ancient symbol, is relatively new as a Jewish symbol. Although it has occasionally been found on remains of early synagogues or tombstones, it appears with more frequency in non-Jewish environments, and five-pointed stars appear at least as often on Jewish objects.

The *magen David* developed into a representative Jewish symbol after the seventeenth century. It was adopted by the First Zionist Congress in 1897 as a symbol for Zionism, precisely because it had no religious overtones but had a great deal of popular appeal and immediate acceptance based on its history as a magical sign, and because it had become widespread during the previous three centuries as an identifying symbol for the Jewish people. Theodor Herzl, the founder of Zionism, thought of emblazoning seven golden stars on a white ground as a flag, the seven stars representing the seven golden hours of labor. But Herzl's friend David Wolffsohn conceived the idea of centering the Star of David on the *tallit* [prayer shawl] as a flag. This design was accepted by the Congress as the Zionist flag; later it was the flag of the Jewish Brigade when it fought in World War II; it was finally adopted as the flag of the modern State of Israel. Thus the Roman robe, the *pallium*, that the Jew wore into exile in the first century of the Common Era, which was preserved as a sacred ritual garment when it was no longer fashionable to wear as common dress, emerged from the *tallit* bag to fly as a national emblem with the newest of the Jewish symbols in its center.

The *magen David* was sanctified in a baptism of fire by the Nazis. Can anyone remain unmoved when he sees, on a beach in Israel, so many young people wearing silver or gold stars of David on their strong bodies? One's mind travels backward to the times when the star was a forced badge of ignominy.

When I was a child, a heart-shaped ten-karat gold locket was the necklace my friends and I dreamed about and asked for on our birthdays, with an expansion bracelet to match if we were lucky. The Jewish Star was something we doodled on the drawings of Christmas trees, which seemed to be the single activity that went on in school from Thanskgiving until December 25. Every day after school, from the third grade on, I went with a few of my friends to a *Yiddishe Shule*. We'd walk down the hill, through the little park, under the elevated tracks (which we nevertheless called the subway) on Southern Boulevard, and over a few blocks to a tiny basement apartment where we learned how to read and write in Yiddish. Almost everyone could speak Yiddish. We were the last of the first-generation children. Hebrew was something esoteric for the *hakhamim* [wisemen]; we were the children of workers, plain people. The only Hebrew word I learned there was *haver* [comrade], which is what we called each other, teachers and students alike. One day in 1948, when I was eleven, we were disturbed at our studies by a tremendous noise in the street right next to our basement windows. Since it was almost time to leave anyway, all the *haverim* went out to the street to see what was happening. It was that time of day when everything is beautiful in the Bronx, even the vegetable-store garbage in the streets. Not quite dark, but all the storefront lights were on so that people could make their last purchases before rushing home for supper. Tired fathers and City College students were being disgorged by the subway into the streets, and since we had been let out of class a few minutes early, it seemed like a holiday. There, on East 173 Street, was a large white truck painted to resemble an ambulance, but on its side, instead of a Red Cross, there was a huge *magen David*. On the hood of the truck stood a young man exhorting the crowd in Yiddish and English to give money and blood to help the new State of Israel. Two flags waved from the truck —the American one to protect the right of free assembly and the new one of blue and white. I was dumbstruck, not so much by what the man was saying but by the truck with its shiny red star. The idea that there could be a *Jewish* ambu-

FIGURE 2: My daughter's bedroom with the quilt in place. Over the bed is a Hebrew *alef-bet* sampler of stitches. The stained-glass *magen David* hanging in the window was given to her when she was born

FIGURE 3: Small white running stitches form a star of David, while quilting together the three layers of the quilt. The cable pattern seen in the white-on-white quilting is an ancient and universal pattern which also appears in the mosaic floor of the sixth-century c.e. Bet Alpha synagogue in the Valley of Jezreel in Israel

lance filled me with profound joy and pride. So, the Star as a symbol for a people, the truck as a symbol of the birth of Zionism (though I still didn't know that word) in the heart of a little girl . . .

When I finished the quilt for my five-year-old daughter's bed, she was delighted but said that it wasn't Jewish (see how I've brainwashed her?). I asked her how we could make it Jewish, and her immediate answer was that we must put "Muben Dubens" on it in some way. My mind and spirit balked at the idea of removing any of the figures and replacing them with star shapes. Then she came up with the idea of quilting the *magen Davids* into the twelve hearts. At this point I can no longer tell if the stars added anything of artistic value to the quilt, but they made her happy, and made me very happy.

Design

❧

BACK IN JUNIOR HIGH SCHOOL, seventh grade I think it was, I had to take a course called "guidance." In it, we decided what our future careers were to be and planned the rest of our academic lives in order to fulfill this master plan. I will refrain from commenting on the educational value of such a course. At one point we had to write essays describing our future profession. I undertook the project with great enthusiasm, describing my projected life as an artist. I filled every possible margin with illustrations, my own drawings, picture postcards, and magazine cuttings. My paper was returned with a huge "F" and the comment: "Order is the First Law of Art." I was dismayed, then furious. I don't remember that teacher's name, but I learned something that day which she had not intended to teach me and which I follow in the classes I teach today: to avoid dogmatic rules in relation to creative work.

I have developed my own ways of designing and sewing. They work for me (most of the time). I can tell you how I have done what I've done and give you a few measurements, but you must trust your own intuition in departing from these designs and in coming up with new ideas. Some people will prefer to make a rough sketch or complete drawing on paper; others prefer to work directly with fabrics and threads. Different approaches to each problem are often utilized. Too often we feel that if we design our own work, rather than use a ready-made design or kit, we are doing something as anarchic and antisocial as designing our own currency, and only others can decide if it is negotiable. This attitude must be combated.

I would like to tell you that designing is easy; that all problems are resolved with no tension; that design is endlessly creative and spontaneous; that decisions are made easily; that trials do not lead to error. But it isn't so. Design, like life, is difficult—but it is not impossible. Once this is recognized you can relax and enjoy yourself. Inhibitions are often the result of the unrealistic desire for, and frustration of, immediate success. The single most important factor in creating a successful design is neither sewing skill nor the ability to draw but simply self-confidence.

Much is made these days of "creativity," "originality," and "self-expression." These have become unattainable goals hysterically sought after. People comb junkyards for unusual materials, or take lessons in one technique after another in their attempt to do something both new and meaningful. They do not realize that the novel and the profound frequently cannot coexist. In this search they tend to overlook their prime resource: themselves, and their own life experiences and cultural heritage.

At the same time that we want to be "creative," we want everything to be fast and easy, not realizing that much of contemporary dissatisfaction exists because our very roles have been made unnecessary by labor-saving devices. We have turned to the crafts to fill the void. It is a natural direction to take, but all too often we want quick results here too. Every desire must be instantly gratified: an heirloom in twenty minutes. I am not opposed to the lessening of time spent on any unpleasant activity, but extending the principal that speed of completion is a positive value to activities that are more enjoyable when savored longer deprives us of a great deal of pleasure. Things done over time incorporate our lives into them. They grow, and we grow with them.

The projects in this book are not complicated; they use simple shapes and basic techniques. They are, however, designed to have a lasting value and so, with a few exceptions, will provide many hours of pleasant work. For me, the element of time sewn into an object enhances its value. The quilt in Figure 2 was made over a four-year period. A great many things happened to our family during that time, and as I worked on the quilt my emotions and thoughts were many and varied. When I look at it now, it seems like a parenthesis enclosing a chapter of my life. It is very precious to my family because they watched it grow and shared in the thrill of its completion in the frantic few days before the fifth birthday of my daughter.

Each creative experience gives birth to another. As you work you will find ideas coming into your head for the next project and the next. Don't let them get away! There is nothing wrong with having many sewing projects going at the same time. That way they can each fill different needs you may have. When you have several quiet hours, that is a good time for designing, cutting, and planning. Waiting in a dentist's office, when major decisions about the project cannot be made, provides the time for the quiet sewing that makes up a good portion of the completed project.

Sometimes we are in an adventurous mood, and the excitement of a fresh beginning is what we want. At other times working quietly on a project in progress has a soothing effect. And then there are days when the satisfaction of bringing something to completion is called for. By having several projects in work simultaneously, you can satisfy your emotional needs in a constructive way.

Sources of inspiration

In designing the projects for this book, I have drawn eclectically from centuries of material and utilized symbols in patterns that are meaningful for me. When turning to tradition for inspiration in creating your own designs, remember that at the times these forms were developing they were *not* traditional, but were contemporary to their era and to the concepts of beauty then prevalent. We can never go back to the idealized past; it wasn't that way in the first place. You may take your inspiration from the past, and even borrow a few ideas and forms (call it "tradition," not "plagiarism"), but allow yourself the freedom to change and adapt them to suit your own life.

Everything is based on something that came before. Even if we work directly from nature, the outcome is influenced by the work of others that we have observed over the years. Individual "style" develops when you have a large enough body of work so that you are drawing from your own previous creations.

The Jews have produced objects in so many diverse environments throughout the Diaspora that no one style is considered to be Jewish. Jewish motifs and themes have been interpreted in so many different ways that we have a rich and varied heritage from which to draw. A round *hallah* cover (Fig. 72) is based on a German eighteenth-century engraved pewter plate which, in turn, drew its inspiration from a book of *minhagim* [customs] printed in Utrecht in 1663.

The *Mazzal Tov* Doll (Fig. 68) is based on the interpretation of the zodiac symbol for the month of Sivan in the mosaic floor of the sixth-century Bet Alpha Synagogue in the Valley of Jezreel in Israel. In both cases one medium was translated into another.

The designs of many ancient mosaic floors and walls which have only recently come to light, and have been made available through books on archaeology and picture postcards, are an excellent source of Jewish design motifs. The simplified shapes lend themselves especially well to interpretations in needlepoint and appliqué.

If you do not live near a city that has a collection of Judaica, you can glean ideas from books available through a synagogue library, a public library (try the travel or archaeology section, as well as the religion section), travel agency brochures for Israel, or your children's Sunday School books. I mention all these as visual aids. For while the Bible and other writings inspire us, it is often difficult for beginners to embody their ideas in an appropriate form.

How to begin

It can be destructive to begin with a clean piece of paper and the expectation that everything will spring fully developed from your head. Start with what you already have or can easily obtain and then work around that.

Rather than sewing something and having it framed—often at unbelievable cost—it might be more fun to find an old frame and design something for it. Although old frames have become increasingly expensive in recent years, unusual shapes or odd sizes are often less costly because they do not easily lend themselves to paintings and prints. Starting with an oval or elliptical frame can give you ideas for composition and scale, and you will have a unique object when you have finished.

Old mirror frames from discarded bedroom dressers can be easily converted for use with objects you are making. The shape and size of the appliqué of two brothers (Fig. 131) was determined by the frame I had bought several weeks earlier at a garage sale. If you begin your embroidery before you find a frame, allow several inches of extra fabric around the edges, and, when a suitable frame turns up, you can trim the fabric to fit and add an additional border or motif if necessary.

Fabrics themselves can beg to be made into something. So don't let the "I can't draw" inhibition keep you from starting a project. Wander around a fabric department, vaguely thinking of cushions or tablecloths or whatever. Touch the fabric, ask a question here and there so it looks as if you are buying something. It may take several such visits, but don't give up. Eventually some fabric will attach itself to you, and you will find thread and other notions that complement it.

Children are a marvelous source of inspiration. Their drawings are usually fresh and spontaneous. They seem to find the essential form of things with a greater clarity of vision than we have. Perhaps it is because, as Wordsworth said, "Heaven lies about us in our infancy," and children, being more recently born, are closer to divine inspiration and intuition. You might ask your child to draw for you, or borrow a neighbor's child. While it might be fun to embroider directly from their drawings, I think children's drawings are best used as beginnings for their own projects. By studying them, however, you can

FIGURE 4: A four-year-old's impression of Israel. The spindly legs, curving neck, humps, and long eyelashes "to keep the sand out" portray the essence of camels perhaps better than a photograph would. Notice the texture on the trunks of the palm trees

FIGURE 5: This 8″ round *hallah* cover was made so my daughter could "play Shabbat." She pretends to light candles in a small pair of brass candlesticks and shares the "*hallah*" (a roll or some cookies) with her dolls and friends. The miniature cloth uses some of the same design elements used on the large cloth which is its companion (Fig. 72)

FIGURE 6: Framed paper-cut incorporating lions

see how they arrive at their simplified interpretations of what they see. It is marvelous to be as free and spontaneous as a child, but I don't imagine we want to be really childish.

Making something for children can be equally instructive, because in order to appeal to them it is necessary to simplify and to use direct shapes and strong color relationships. The meticulous niceties that you might worry about in relation to a tea-table cloth are of no concern at all to the more direct mind of a child. Miniatures of adult objects have great appeal to children and are a good way for you to develop expertise.

Another way of beginning a design is to use cut-paper shapes. Cut-out work (in bark, parchment, fabric, and paper) has been done in many cultures throughout the world and has existed for thousands of years. It was a technique used in the Jewish communities of Holland and Italy in the seventeenth, eighteenth, and early nineteenth centuries to decorate the border of parchment *ketubot* [marriage contracts] and *megillot* [scrolls] of the Book of Esther. As paper became readily available, paper-cuts became a universal medium for folk art. Jewish paper-cuts were very popular in Hungary, Poland, Russia, and North Africa in the nineteenth and early twentieth centuries. Round paper-cuts were made to decorate the small village windowpanes during the late-spring holiday of Shavuot [Pentecost], and many were made as protective amulets to be hung in the room of a new mother and her baby. The most common type of paper-cut was made as an ornament for the eastern wall, the *mizrah* [east], of the home so that anyone entering would know in which direction to face when praying, since for most Jews of the world the Land of Israel is to the east. They were often painted with watercolors and framed under glass. The designs for the lion on the needlepoint *tallit* bag, the felt appliqué frame, the crewel *mizrah*, and the double *hallah* cover (Figs. 63, 121, 114, and 76) were all started by me as paper-cuts. The lion and the crewel embroidery were based on paper-cuts I had done as *mizrahim*, and the other two from paper-cuts made with the specific objects in mind.

The nice thing about paper-cuts is that you don't have to be able to draw in order to get very pleasing results. The paper is folded in half or fourths, and a few shapes drawn on one section of the folded paper. Connecting lines (e.g., scrolls, vines, etc.) are added to keep everything from falling apart when the paper-cut is unfolded. The design is cut out using a manicure or embroidery scissors. Parts of the design may be cut apart and used separately.

If you do start your design with a drawing, you might want to try cutting out the shape you have drawn and placing it on a contrasting sheet of paper just to see if the form is as well defined as it might be. A very pleasant way to compose a design is to cut the shapes you are using—whether letters or objects—out of paper and to move them around on your background fabric until you have made an arrangement that pleases you.

If you want some of the shapes in their mirror image, it is a simple matter to use the cut-out as a pattern and cut another, which you then use in a reverse position. When you have a satisfying arrangement, draw around each shape onto the background cloth and proceed with your embroidery. If the design is to be appliquéd, use the paper patterns to cut out the shapes from cloth.

Color

Color is another possible point of departure for creating a design. You can begin with the desire to make something in a particular color, or because the color of some fabric that your aunt brought you from Thailand is so inviting, or because the color of a certain flower or birthstone has a special meaning for you. Pick colors that you like and that make you feel good, rather than going by someone else's notion of what "matches."

Too often in kits we see color combinations that try to please everyone. In an attempt to gain excitement, they pretend to duplicate nature by using a multicolor design. By carefully observing natural phenomena, however, you will notice that the most inspiring effects are achieved by the Master with a very limited palette: a snowy morning when only a few dark tree trunks define the landscape; a sunset or sunrise that is a brilliant swatch of golds, oranges, and pinks, luminous against grayed-out mountains; a summer day that is a study in greens; or a foggy morning in the winter woods.

Decide whether you want the finished effect to be subtle or dramatic. If you opt for subtlety, choose monochromatic shades of one color, with or without a small accent in a contrasting color. If you prefer a dramatic effect, use colors that contrast strongly. A light color on a dark background is often more dramatic than a dark design on a light background. Here are some ways of arriving at color schemes:

Strong contrast: your favorite bright color on white. Or white on any dark color: violet, dark brown, olive or forest green, for example

Two tones of the same color

Two tones of the same color plus black and/or white

Two tones of the same color plus one contrasting color

Three or more shades of one color

Three or more shades of one color plus one contrasting color plus white

You will notice that this list proceeds from the simplest (though very effective) types of color combinations to the more complex.

Colors harmonize if they have something in common; they are discordant if they do not. It is easier to successfully combine colors that contain some of the same hue, such as yellow with yellowish-green and yellowish-blue. Like people, colors are affected by their environment. Two blues in a red background will look the same, while a composition of only blue tones will show the subtle differences in intensity (brightness) and value (the amount of dark or light) of each shade of blue. Try for balance in the distribution of color in your design. Imagine a transparent geometrical figure over your design and place spots of your strongest color at the corners.

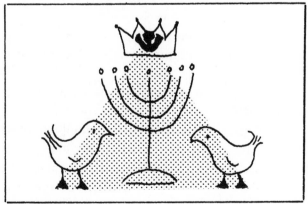

FIGURE 7: Spots of the same color were placed at the three angles of an imaginary triangle

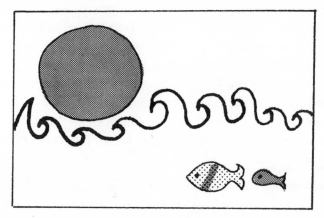

FIGURE 8: The same color has been repeated in the sun, the small fish, and the stripe of the large fish

In asymmetrical designs, a large colored shape can be balanced by several smaller shapes in the same or a closely related color.

Many objects are associated with a particular color. The naturalistic colors can be used as a basis for design. Or by using totally different colors, unusual meanings can be added to an ordinary object. Psychological associations with color are at least as important in artwork as naturalistic representation. Red is associated with energy, ferocity, blood, and bloodshed. It is this last association that makes red the only color I know of that has a rabbinic prohibition associated with it: the straps of the *tefillin* [phylacteries] can be made of any color but red (these days they are usually made in black). With this one exception, any and all colors can be used to make Jewish objects.

There is widespread Jewish identification with the combination of blue and white. This identification is as ancient as the Jewish people itself. It is specified in Numbers 15:37–41 that the Hebrews should include a thread of blue in the fringes ritually tied at the four corners of their garments. The fringe with its thread of blue is to serve as a constant reminder to follow the commandments and to "be holy unto your God." Scholars have long debated as to which was of greater significance, the fringe itself or the blue color. Blue represents the sea and the sky. All life emerged from the waters, and continues to be wholly dependent upon it. Teeming with life, the sea—and therefore the color blue—has powerful associations with fertility. Brides wear "something blue." The sky is associated with heaven and the dwelling place of the Deity and the angels. Blue then becomes a profoundly symbolic color uniting the earthly and heavenly forces. Other Middle Eastern peoples continue to use blue as a magical device to keep away the "evil eye" by commonly painting houses (particularly window surrounds) and even cars in shades of blue. For Jews, however, the power of blue lies in its capacity to turn us toward a consecrated life.

In ancient times the shade of blue used for the ritual fringe was made from a dye obtained from a particular shellfish, so rare that, even then, imitation vegetable or mineral dyes were sometimes foisted off on the unsuspecting purchaser. Because of the difficulty in securing the "true blue," the early rabbis concluded that it was preferable to skip the blue thread altogether. The discussion as to whether or not to include a blue thread in the ritual fringes continues to this day.

While blue did not appear in the ritual fringes for great periods of time, it was often used for the bands at either end of the *tallit*. Its celestial associations remained in the Jewish mind, and blue took a place of honor again on the Zionist flag, which is now the flag of the State of Israel, as a constant reminder of the high calling of the Covenant People Israel to serve as a "light unto the nations."

Talmudic legend relates that when Moses went up to heaven he found the angels clothed in the colors of the Tabernacle. Foremost among the angels were those wearing blue. Blue is the first color specified by God for use in the design and construction of the desert Sanctuary. The other colors used were purple, scarlet, and white, and I chose this color combination for the five articles for the Pesah Seder (Figs. 93, 95, 98, 99, 102). Since Pesah commemorates our freedom from Egyptian bondage, the very colors listed in Exodus 25 were an ideal choice. The color combination seems very contemporary, yet it is so old. The other, traditionally styled Pesah *matzah* cover (Fig. 104) was made with green silk thread on a white background. Green is associated with growth, peace, and plenty, and Passover comes in the spring when the world is just beginning to turn green again.

As for the other colors of the Tabernacle: purple connotes power and royalty, and white, purity, both admirable qualities for the dwelling of the Divine Spirit. As for the scarlet (and red-dyed ram skins), we know that the emerging Hebrew nation was not always pacific, and often had need of a Lord of Hosts. Red also has associations with warmth and curative powers. It has been a popular color for winter underclothes, and a piece of red flannel wrapped around the neck is still thought by many to have a beneficial effect on a sore throat. Perhaps this goes back to the biblical idea of a good homemaker who "is not afraid of the snow for her household; For her household are clothed with scarlet" (Proverbs 31:21).

Gold, silver, and copper, as well as various woods and animal skins, were also used in the Tabernacle, and their colors are eminently suitable for Jewish art objects. Gold symbolizes light as the spirit of the Divine; silver denotes holiness. Golds, yellows, and wood-tones combine successfully for almost any kind of embroidery, from the most traditional to the very modern.

It might seem that this discussion about the symbolic values of color is from some dark, magic-oriented past, but recent research in factories, schools, and mental institutions has shown that different colors produce strikingly different emotional reactions.

Patchwork sampler

In the past, people learned by doing things with their hands. I believe this is still a valid way to learn. All the diagrams, explanations, and demonstrations cannot teach one as much as sitting quietly and experimenting with needles, thread, and fabric.

Doing a sampler is a marvelous way to learn sewing techniques. A sampler gives the sewer familiarity with many stitches and with how they work for specific fabrics and designs. What usually comes to mind when we hear the word "sampler" is a piece of linen embroidered in cross stitch with an inspiring or sentimental quotation in the middle. Originally, samplers served as "sourcebooks" for designs. If someone had an idea, or saw one worth borrowing, she noted it down on her sampler, which was usually a long narrow strip of fabric. Since it was meant as a notebook, no attempt at composition was made, and designs were not repeated. Later, samplers were used to demonstrate the different stitches a young girl had mastered and her talent at combining them into a pleasant design: a final exam, so to speak, after years of practice. In colonial America, children started to sew at ages when they are now considered too young to enter kindergarten. By the time a child was nine or ten, she was often an accomplished embroideress, and the sampler served to demonstrate her skill. Since most of us have not been sewing from such an early age and will probably want to learn stitches and techniques while creating something useful, I would like to suggest a kind of sampler that will provide a learning experience in the making and will, at the same time, be a decorative item.

Before beginning any of the projects in this book, you might cut a small patch of the fabric you will be working on and use it to practice the stitches and to become familiar with the motifs of the design. Sample patches for different projects should be multiples of sizes which later will combine easily into a single patchwork design. Mine, for example, is all done in multiples of three inches. Therefore some of the units are 3″ squares, others 6″ squares, rectangles of 3″ x 6″, 6″ x 9″, etc. Allow an additional ⅜″ or ½″ all around as your seam allowance. Then some day, when you have enough of these little patches for a cushion, a wall hanging, or a baby- or child-size quilt, assemble them as though you were playing with blocks. Add patches of colored or patterned fabric cut in these same measurement multiples. If you still don't have enough, add a big border. In any case, you'll have a pleasant record of your experiments with stitches and with Jewish motifs.

FIGURE 9: Patchwork sampler in progress using motifs from projects in this book

FIGURE 10: Patchwork sampler made as a wall hanging by twenty-five
Sunday School children

Stitches

THE SIMPLEST STITCHES offer the most possibilities for variation and development. Just as one person's handwriting is different from another's, the same stitches have a different character depending upon who makes them. There is no such thing as "too tight" or "too loose." One person sews with disciplined regularity, while her friend will never have two running stitches that are the same. The important thing is that you work in a manner comfortable for you, with or without a thimble or embroidery hoop.

While there are hundreds of embroidery stitches, most of them are variations of the basic ones used in this book. I find the simplest stitches adequate to my needs. Diagrams of these follow. Refer to them when you need to, but always feel free to replace the stitch I have used in a design with one that is more appealing to you.

BUTTONHOLE STITCH

The buttonhole stitch and its variations are useful for finishing edges and hems as well as for purely ornamental purposes. The stitch can be worked in either direction, the spaces and vertical lines varied. It was used to edge the hearts on the quilt in Figure 2.

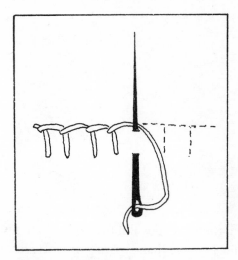

FIGURE 11: Buttonhole stitch

Closed buttonhole stitches are made in pairs forming triangles. It is used for appliqué here in Figure 14.

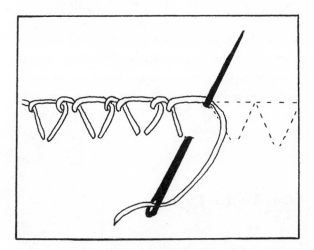

FIGURE 12: Closed buttonhole stitch

The alternating buttonhole stitch is used here to join the two pieces of fabric.

FIGURE 13: Alternating buttonhole stitch

4: Closed buttonhole stitch used as appliqué

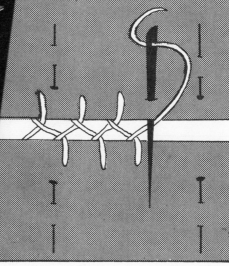

CHAIN STITCH

The chain stitch is attractive worked in any type of yarn. While it is most often used for linear designs and inscriptions, it can also be used as a filling stitch by making several rows close to one another until the shape is complete.

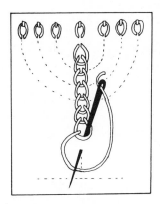

FIGURE 15: Chain stitch

FIGURE 16: Chain stitch is used to outline the amulet-type hand. The design is filled in with a lazy daisy stitch flower, straight stitches, and threaded running stitches

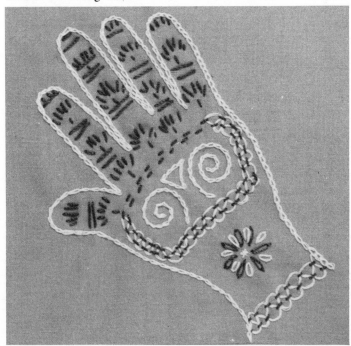

COUCHING

Couching is a technique with an enormous range of possible uses. Three types of couching are shown here.

Linear Couching

Any stitch used to secure another thread in place is called a couching stitch. Here a heavy thread is couched in place with a simple overcast stitch, using a thinner thread in a contrasting color. Tiny cross stitches may also be used. In Yemenite embroidery, gold and silver cords are couched in place with tiny, almost invisible stitches securing the cord in complex designs.

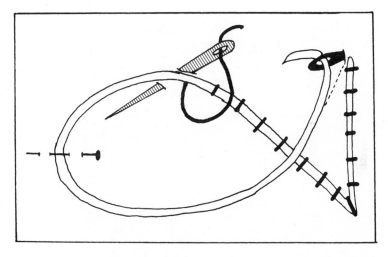

FIGURE 17: Linear couching

Couched Trellis Filling

Long diagonal threads are secured where they intersect with small running stitches. A trellis effect can also be made using horizontal and vertical lines rather than diagonal lines.

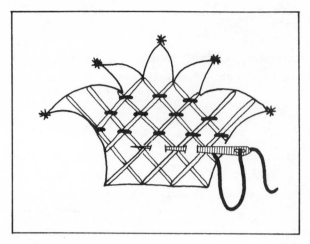

FIGURE 18: Couched trellis filling

Laid-and-Couched Filling

This can also be called the "Bayeaux Tapestry stitch," since the Bayeaux Tapestry (which is really an embroidery on linen rather than a woven tapestry) was worked almost entirely in it.

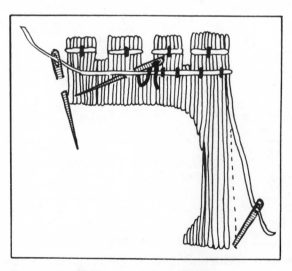

FIGURE 19: Laid-and-couched filling

Filling a shape with laid-and-couched work is a three-step procedure. First, long surface satin stitches are made to completely fill in the desired shape. Six strands of embroidery floss works well for this. Surface satin stitches differ from regular satin stitches in that the thread does not go from one side of the design to the other on the reverse side of the fabric. This would use too much thread and be too bulky. Rather, a tiny stitch is picked up between each long stitch. It is essential to use a hoop for this stitch to keep the stitches flat and taut. In filling a large shape, it is easier to begin in the middle and work toward one end; then, starting at the middle again, work toward the other end. The second step is to place long, spaced stitches across the laid work. This can be done in simple, straight lines, or a trellis can be made. Finally, these holding stitches are secured in place. This can be done, as indicated here, with an overcasting stitch or with other, more decorative stitches. For greater definition, go around the edge of the shape in outline or chain stitch. For a variety of effects, it is possible to use a different color for each step of the stitch.

FIGURE 20: Laid-and-couched work fill in the letter *tav*. Buttonhole stitch is used for the letter *shin*. The ornaments on both letters are satin stitch

CRETAN STITCH

The Cretan stitch gives a zigzag effect, but it is done with the needle always in a horizontal position. The stitches can be made very close together for a braidlike filling. Cretan stitch also makes an attractive border.

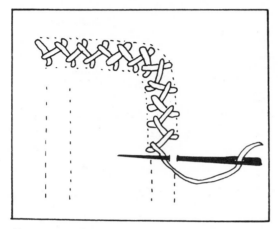

FIGURE 21: Cretan stitch

FIGURE 22: Cretan stitch forms a thick line

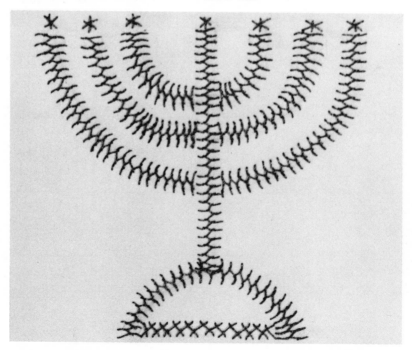

CROSS STITCH

Each cross stitch can be made separately, or, as is shown here, a complete row of diagonal stitches may be made first and the crosses completed on the return trip.

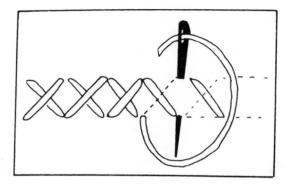

FIGURE 23: Cross stitch

The double cross stitch involves superimposing a cross stitch made with vertical and horizontal lines over one made with diagonal lines. Stitches will usually be more even if each double cross is made individually.

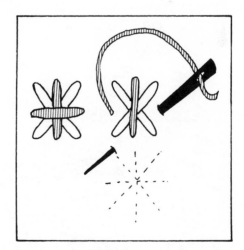

FIGURE 24: Double cross stitch

FEATHER STITCH

The feather stitch begins with a "Y." The feather is created by swinging the stitches alternately to either side of a stem. Many variations are possible by changing the length and spacing of the stitches and by making additional loops on one side or the other.

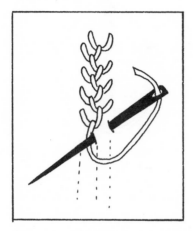

FIGURE 25: Feather stitch

FIGURE 26: Feather stitch used as a decorative edge for appliqué

FISHBONE OR LEAF STITCH

This stitch can be made to conform to almost any shape of leaf. When it is worked in a fine thread, it has a very lacy appearance, while with coarser yarn it is very sturdy-looking.

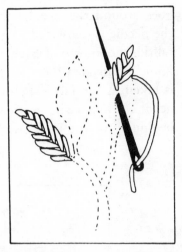

FIGURE 27: Fishbone or leaf stitch

HERRINGBONE STITCH

The herringbone stitch and its many variations are useful for borders, fillings, linear designs, and appliqué.

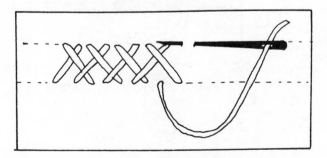

FIGURE 28: Herringbone stitch

KNOTS

Knots are made by winding the thread around the needle before reinserting it in the fabric. The more times the thread goes around the needle, the bigger the knot becomes. When the needle is reinserted very close to where it emerged from the fabric, the knot will have a round shape and is called a French knot. To make a long, narrow bullion knot, a large back stitch is taken in the fabric before the thread is wrapped around the needle. The needle is then reinserted into the fabric at the beginning of the back stitch.

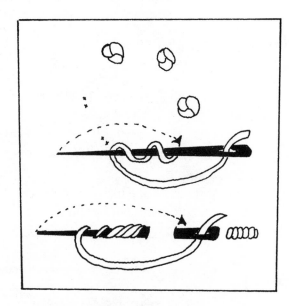

FIGURE 29: French and bullion knots

LAZY DAISY STITCH

Each petal-shaped lazy daisy stitch is really a detached chain stitch. It is useful for embroidering flowers, small leaves, or flames.

FIGURE 30: Lazy daisy

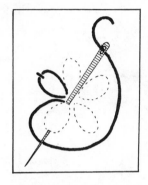

LONG-AND-SHORT STITCH

The greatest success is achieved with this stitch if it is not done too evenly. It is made up of rows of stitches that are alternately long and short, the long stitches of the second row filling in the spaces left by the short ones of the first row. This stitch is often used where shaded effects are desired.

FIGURE 31: Long-and-short stitch

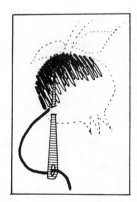

OUTLINE OR STEM STITCH

The outline stitch, or stem stitch as it is sometimes known, is one of the most useful stitches in the vocabulary of embroidery. It can be used for any type of linear design and makes a very attractive filling when many rows of it are worked close together.

FIGURE 32: Outline or stem stitch

RUNNING STITCH

The running stitch is the most basic of all stitches and probably the first one we learn as children. Because it is so simple, its decorative possibilities are often neglected. I have used it throughout this book for embroidery as well as appliqué and quilting.

Two ways of threading running stitches are shown here, but the possibilities are limitless. Threaded running stitches make simple and decorative borders.

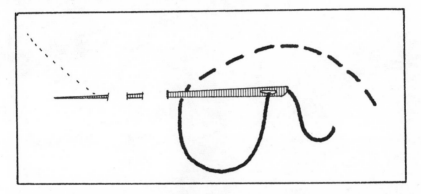

FIGURE 33: Running stitch and two threaded running stitches

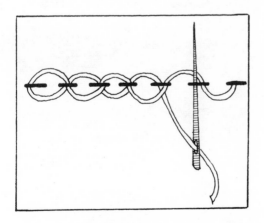
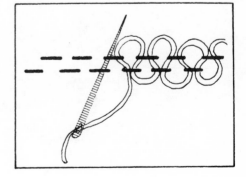

FIGURE 34: Running stitches are used to hold the felt shapes in place and for decorative details

SATIN STITCH

The satin stitch is very popular for filling in small shapes. Because it has a tendency to pucker the material, it is suggested that you use a hoop for this stitch.

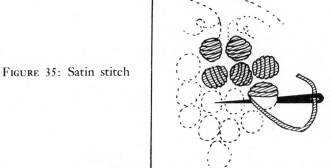

FIGURE 35: Satin stitch

STRAIGHT STITCH

The straight stitch is a single spaced stitch which can be made in any desired direction and size. It is advisable, however, not to have the stitches overly long or loose. As shown here, straight stitches can be made to conform to simple patterns.

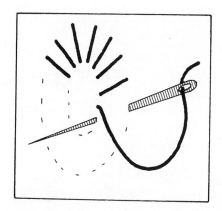

FIGURE 36: Straight stitch

APPLIQUÉ WITH BLIND STITCH

The important characteristic of the blind stitch is that it is very short on top of the material (indeed, it can sometimes be almost invisible). Distance is covered between the stitches on the back of the work. The stitches are made right at the edge of the shape. The finished bird shape is indicated by the dotted line, which is the fold line. Notice that the seam allowance is clipped at the concave curves and cut away at the sharp corners. Sometimes notches are cut at convex curves. This trimming is to eliminate excess bulk. Clip as little as possible, since it weakens the fabric, but as much as necessary to insure smoothness. The shape to be appliquéd is pinned in place, and the pins adjusted and removed as the stitching proceeds.

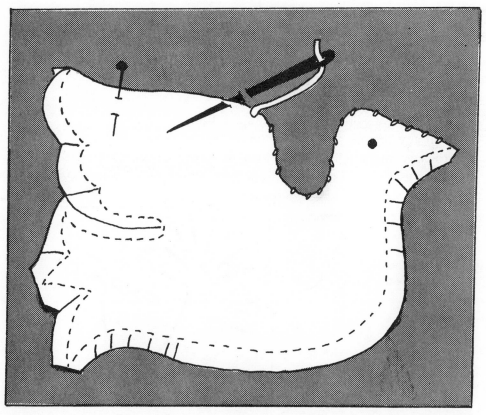

FIGURE 37: Blind stitch used for appliqué

FIGURE 38: The blind stitch is the stitch most often used for appliqué. Note the herringbone stitch used for the "grass"

Stitches for canvas work

BASKETWEAVE TENT STITCH

The basketweave is a little more difficult to master than the other tent stitches such as the continental and the half cross, but, once learned, its advantages are worth the extra effort. It gives the work a smooth appearance and distorts the canvas far less than the other stitches; it is also very pleasant to work. Because of the characteristic woven effect on the back of the canvas (which gives the stitch its name), it is exceptionally durable.

FIGURE 39: Detail of the Lion and the Dove *tallit* bag showing the basketweave tent stitch used for the face and background, the upright cross stitch for the mane, and a checkerboard body made with alternate squares of tent and Scotch stitches

The basketweave stitch is worked in parallel, diagonal rows. The first row is a single corner stitch in the upper right-hand corner. Each subsequent row is one stitch longer than the preceding row. For the ascending rows, the needle is held in a horizontal position and goes under two canvas threads. For the descending rows, the needle is held vertically and also goes under two canvas threads before making the diagonal stitch.*

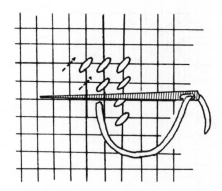

FIGURE 40: The basketweave tent stitch, ascending and descending

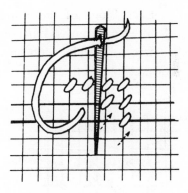

* It is very important to alternate one ascending row and one descending row, as two rows worked in the same direction will cause a slight ridge. (This is not visible, however, when you change colors between rows.) If you are uncertain about the direction of your last row, turn the canvas over and look at the back: if the stitches appear horizontal, it was an ascending row; if they are vertical, a descending row.

B R I C K   S T I T C H

The brick pattern is made by alternating the stitches in each row. The length of the stitches can be varied, but are usually done over even-number threads (2, 4, 6, etc.). The stitch can be worked horizontally or vertically. Notice that in order to even up the first row, half-length stitches are made.

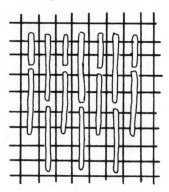

FIGURE 41: Brick stitch

S C O T C H   S T I T C H

Each block of the Scotch stitch is made up of five stitches of different lengths. Different colors can be used for alternating squares or within each square itself. For a more pronounced checkerboard effect, the alternate squares can be worked with nine tent stitches.

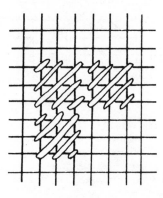

FIGURE 42: Scotch stitch

UPRIGHT CROSS STITCH

In order to achieve the characteristic nubby effect of this stitch, each cross must be completed before going on to the next stitch. It provides a pleasant, small-scale textural contrast when worked with the tent stitch.

FIGURE 43: Upright cross stitch

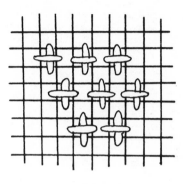

Supplies, Tools,
and Techniques

Fabrics and threads

JEWISH EMBROIDERY is distinguishable from other sewing by its function and subject matter and by its adherence to the rule of *shaatnez* ["mingling of the fibers"]. The mixing of linen and wool is prohibited by the Bible (Leviticus 19:19; Deuteronomy 22:11). This prohibition applies to garments, articles made for warmth, and upholstery fabric.

The first chapter of Genesis, where plant, marine, and animal species are created, each with distinctive characteristics "after its kind," is often cited in attempts to explain this statute. Some commentators have deduced that "Nature does not rejoice in the union of things that are not in their nature alike" (Josephus). Another explanation which is often given is that the law was instituted to protect the unsuspecting buyer from being cheated with an inferior mixture of linen and wool when he thought he was buying pure wool. Still other scholars see this rule as having originated as a religious taboo: since the garments of the priests contained both linen and wool, this mixture was prohibited for use by laymen.

57

None of these explanations is completely satisfying. However, since the *shaatnez* prohibition is explicitly stated in the Bible, Orthodox Jews interpret it as a divine decree whose purpose is to safeguard the physical universe according to the natural laws established by the Creator, but whose full meaning may be outside the realm of human knowledge and understanding. *Shaatnez* is, therefore, one of the few biblical laws meant to be accepted on faith alone. Many Jews are completely unaware of this statute, but in Orthodox communities there are often laboratories available that test fabric to ascertain its fiber content.

If you are not Orthodox yourself, it would be advisable to keep *shaatnez* in mind when making a gift for someone who is. Since there is such a wide range of fabrics available today, and synthetics come in an enormous variety of textures and colors, observing *shaatnez* presents no real limitation to the creation of beautiful embroideries.

A visit to a fabric store is a visual and tactile treat. But after looking at and touching all the sumptuous and textured fabrics, I always seem to choose a medium-weight cotton fabric with a linenlike weave (or linen) for my embroidery projects. I find this type of fabric very pleasant to work with. Usually it is not too difficult to find cotton batiste lining in a matching color for lining fabric. The simpler and more basic the fabric, the more involved I become in its embellishment. Unless you are sewing exclusively by machine, avoid fabric with a very close, hard weave, as it is very difficult to push a needle through. Loosely woven fabric, such as burlap, is suitable for certain wall hangings and draperies but not for table linen or anything receiving hard wear or requiring frequent laundering.

While it is possible to sew with anything linear and pliable —such as fishing line, leather strips, and metal wire—the threads used in this book are the conventional ones commonly found in local shops. If you have access to unusual yarns and enjoy experimenting, please do. Yarns sold especially for embroidery or darning are usually the most pleasant to work with.

Knitting yarn is often too soft for embroidery unless it is couched in place. But for sewing with wool, crewel, tapestry, or darning yarn is suggested.

I used to work with embroidery floss almost exclusively, but after using some cotton pearl thread for a matching crochet border, I began using it for embroidery as well and find it very enjoyable and easy to work with. It comes in two weights, in the same shades as embroidery thread. Mercerized cotton is suggested for appliqué work, though embroidery floss is more decorative if you are using ornamental stitches rather than blind stitches.

Needles

In choosing a needle for embroidery it is important to select one that is comfortable in your hand, is easy to thread, and will not leave large holes in the fabric. Sharp-pointed crewel needles are used for general embroidery, while blunt-tipped tapestry needles are used for canvas work. The crewel needle differs from an ordinary "sharp" needle by having a larger eye, enabling more strands of thread to fit through it. The lower the number of the needle, the bigger it is. I find a No. 7 crewel needle suitable for almost any embroidery and appliqué need. Crewel needles are also sold in packages containing an assortment of needles Nos. 5–9 so you can find the size that suits you best. A No. 18 tapestry needle is the size used most commonly for canvas work. While I prefer hand embroidery because I find it more relaxing, the sewing machine, if properly and sensitively used, can be considered an extension of the hand rather than a mechanistic intrusion.

Scissors

Sewing scissors should be very sharp. It is therefore a good idea not to use the same pair of scissors for fabric and for paper. A sharp-pointed scissor with a 4″ blade will serve all your basic sewing needs. But you might want to expand your tool wardrobe to include pinking shears which help to keep the edges from raveling, large fabric shears to cut heavy fabric, and small embroidery scissors for fine trimming and snipping threads.

Embroidery hoops

Embroidery hoops come in a variety of sizes and shapes in metal or wood. Some people can never accustom themselves to working with a hoop while others cannot manage without one. I find a hoop very useful for some stitches (laid-and-couched, for example) and a bother with others. Rather than using a hoop that encompasses the entire area to be embroidered, I prefer a small 4″ circle or an oval of 4½″ x 9″. I feel as though I have greater control over the embroidery with a small hoop because I can easily get to each stitch. I always use a wooden, rather than metal, hoop because the metal ones (even those lined with cork) have a tendency to leave discoloring marks on the fabric.

Thimbles

For those of you who sew a lot and have tried to use a thimble and found it uncomfortable, I recommend you try a silver thimble. This isn't mere affectation. Silver readily conducts heat and so adapts itself to your finger. Within a few minutes you all but forget you have it on, except for the protection it offers. Thimbles come in many sizes, so make sure it fits properly. For general use, do not get the heavily ornamented silver thimbles from Mexico, which are shown in many gift shops, as these catch on everything. They are fun to collect, but not very practical. Good fabric and sewing shops will usually have silver thimbles if you ask for them. I have one with a synthetic stone in the tip which is especially good for quilting.

Techniques and procedures

With some projects, you may choose to work without a drawing by cutting and pinning shapes of cloth and experimenting with stitches, thereby letting the design grow along with the work. For others, a small, rough sketch will be sufficient. Some projects, on the other hand, will require that the complete drawing be worked out to scale on paper before you begin. Since most of the projects in the book are bigger than ordinary typing or notebook paper, wrapping paper or shelf paper may come in handy. Heavy brown paper is useful for cutting patterns. Shelf paper, while strong, is often thin enough to be somewhat transparent when you need mirror images, and it is easily used with dressmaker's carbon paper for transferring the drawing to the fabric.

ENLARGING A PATTERN OR DRAWING

The simplest way to enlarge a drawing or pattern is to bring it to a photo-processing shop where any black-and-white drawing can be enlarged or reduced to almost any size rapidly and inexpensively. If a shop that performs this service is not available in your locality, the grid method can be used.

GRID METHOD

On a large sheet of paper, draw the outside measurements of your proposed embroidery. Draw intersecting lines, horizontally and vertically, spacing the lines 1″ apart. Count the number of squares thus created, and draw a grid with the same number of squares over your pattern-drawing. If the pattern already has a grid over it, make sure that the grid on your paper contains the same number of squares. Then copy the pattern, one square at a time. If it is a complex design, it will be helpful to have someone assist you in keeping your place. Start in one corner and work systematically by rows to avoid missing any of the squares.

PUTTING THE DESIGN ON FABRIC

When drawing on fabric, care must be taken to use a writing instrument that will show up sufficiently, will not easily be brushed away, and will not bleed into the fabric or threads while you are sewing or later in the laundry.

Designs can be drawn directly on the fabric with an ordinary sharp pencil. Draw lightly and remove any inaccurate lines with a kneaded eraser. This is a type of eraser used by draftsmen; it is available where art and school supplies are sold. If your design is drawn on paper, use dressmaker's tracing paper (not ordinary carbon paper, which smears) to transfer the drawing. A light coat of charcoal-fixative spray will keep the design from rubbing off as you sew. Use the type of fixative that is called "workable." This has a nonglossy surface and does not change the quality of the fabric. By the time you have finished sewing, it will be worn away. Spraying with this type of fixative is also helpful if you draw with tailor's pencils or chalk.

There are many materials available for putting designs on canvas. Indelible ink, felt-tip pens, India ink (it comes in colors as well as in black), and acrylic paints are all useful. If you make a mistake on canvas, cover it with white paint or with typewriter correction fluid. Since the yarn will cover everything, the most important thing to keep in mind is that the pigment must be permanent and not bleed into the yarn. Spray it lightly with a fixative described above, which can generally be found in art-supply or hobby shops.

FINISHING

When the embroidery is finished, it should be ironed with a steam iron or by placing a dampened cloth over the embroidery. Pad the ironing board with towels and place the embroidery face down over the padding; this keeps the stitches from becoming flattened.

Specific directions are given in this book for finishing each project. Several of these require mitered corners in order to lie flat. A mitered corner is one that is constructed with a diagonal seam in the following manner:

1) turn under the corner point of the seam allowance, making a diagonal fold across the corner of the fabric;

2) fold each adjoining edge halfway over the diagonal fold, forming a new point;

3) slip stitch the two folded edges together;

4) trim away excess fabric.

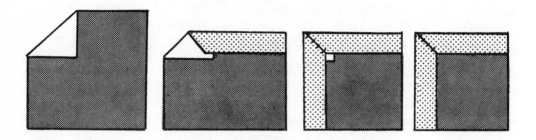

FIGURE 44: Mitering corners

TWO

THE PROJECTS

Patchwork

IN THE FIFTH GRADE at P.S. 61, Colonial America came alive for me. Every year, in all the preceding grades, we had drawn Thanksgiving turkeys and made tall black construction-paper Puritan hats. Somehow that was "theirs," not mine. In the fifth grade, though, in the inevitable chapter on the colonists, the text described pioneer women and girls weaving cloth from home-grown fibers. After making all the family clothes, they saved the still-usable scraps of leftover fabric and, for relaxation and diversion, pieced them together into quilts. At last here was something American I could really identify with. As Hawthorne says in *The Scarlet Letter*, "Women derive a pleasure, incomprehensible to the other sex, from the delicate toil of the needle." It unites in wordless companionship women from all corners of the earth, from all stations of life, bridging gaps in history and in language.

Religion played a vital role in the lives of the Puritans. They identified with the biblical Hebrews, feeling that they had left a land alien to their religious convictions and had, after much travail, arrived in the Promised Land. Early American quilt patterns were often biblically inspired, with names such as "David and Goliath," "King David's Crown," "Garden of Eden," "Children of Israel," "Job's Troubles," "Job's Tears," "Rose of Sharon," "Joseph's Coat," and "Jacob's Ladder." Many of these old patterns were traditionally made in blue and white, a further indication of the Puritans' close reading of the Old Testament in which the Hebrews are enjoined to include a thread of blue in the corner fringes of their garments so that they "may look upon it, and remember all the commandments of the Lord" (Numbers 15:37–41).

As the country grew, it changed in character, and the traditional quilt patterns took on new names: "Jacob's Ladder," one of the most attractive of the biblical designs, became "Wagon Tracks" in Mississippi, "Trail of the Covered Wagon" in the prairie states, "The Underground Railroad" in western Kentucky. This is but another example of how an old and powerful symbol is retained while its interpretation changes.

Although most of America's Jews are part of a later immigration, they too look back to the early New England settlements as part of the heritage they have in common with other Americans. Perhaps it is time to dust off some of the old biblical patterns, restore their old names, and thank the Puritans for their "contributions to Jewish art."

Aside from cut-and-pieced quilts, these geometric patterns adapt very well to needlepoint: one square could make a pillow, several together a hanging.

General directions for patchwork

Patchwork relies for its effectiveness on the careful joining of many small pieces of fabric to achieve an exciting overall effect. The regular repetition of simple shapes in well-chosen colors and prints produces designs that can favorably compare with the most intricate geometric abstract.

Some general things to keep in mind are these: unless you are absolutely certain of the compatibility of the various fabrics you are using, launder and press all fabrics before you begin. It is unwise to mix different kinds of fabric. Usually, instead of adding interest, it makes the finished work appear uneven and messy and can cause problems later in laundering. Fabric combinations that are exciting in appliqué can destroy the overall pattern effect of geometric patchwork. Use all corduroy together, or all drapery fabric, or all cotton dressmaking fabric. An exception is the Victorian crazy quilt, which effectively combines velvets, silks, and wools with elaborate embroidery. Synthetic blends that are similar to cotton can be used with cotton fabric. Patchwork is ideal for using up leftover pieces from other domestic sewing projects (or at least turning your still-leftover scraps into smaller ones). We now live in an era when our time is considered to be more valuable than scraps of fabric. Since you will be putting a lot of time, effort, and emotion into your patchwork, I would strongly recommend using all new fabric, and permanently pressed material at that—except, of course, when you are using the material from objects that have special meaning for you, as I did in making the *tallit* bag of my husband's ties (Fig. 57).

In joining the shapes together, the important line is the seam line, not the seam allowance or the cutting line. Therefore, all cardboard patterns should be made the exact size that you want the finished shape to be. Draw carefully around the pattern with a sharp pencil on the reverse side of the fabric. The fabric is then cut ¼" or ⅜" outside of this line. Sew carefully on the pencil line in order to make certain that all the corners meet. When drawing many shapes on fabric at the same time, make certain to leave enough space between them to insure adequate seam allowances. It is not essential to have all the seam allowances identical.

Shapes can be cut out of cardboard or sandpaper for tracing. Sandpaper is recommended because, when placed face down on the fabric for tracing, its rough surface helps to keep the fabric from sliding.

If the shapes are to be seamed together, they are drawn on the reverse side of the material. If they are to be appliquéd, then the drawn line is on the front of the fabric. The pencil line then becomes the fold line when the work is sewn in place.

A sharp pencil is the best thing to use in drawing shapes on most fabrics. This line can be erased later with a kneaded eraser if it shows at all in appliqué. On fabrics such as silk or wool, a pencil may not be visible, so dressmaker's chalk, a waterproof pen, a felt-tip, or even a ballpoint, can be used. Always try to use the one that will show up enough but will not show through the fabric.

FIGURE 45: The finished "Jacob's Ladder" crib quilt. There is a quilt-making tradition that since only God can make a perfect thing, the quiltmaker should make "a mistake" in the design. While most quilt-making books say this custom is of Oriental derivation, it sounds to me like an interpretation of the Second Commandment. The "mistake" is on the right edge, one-third of the way up from the bottom

"*JACOB'S LADDER*" *CRIB QUILT*

The intriguing thing about this pattern is that while each block makes a ladder, when many blocks are combined a secondary, diagonal pattern appears. This pattern makes a very effective wall hanging using as many squares as you desire. One square could be the bib front of a dress, blouse, or apron, while many, depending on your size, could be made up into a long skirt. Curtains, draperies, valances, and cushions could be made to match the quilt if you like pattern in large doses. As you will see later, I have used this pattern for a *tallit* bag of velvet and wool. The crib quilt is made up of twelve 12" squares plus 3" borders.

FINISHED DIMENSIONS: 42" x 54"

MATERIALS:
2 yards blue cotton fabric
2 yards small white print
2 yards dacron quilt batting for filling
2 yards lining material
cotton pearl thread for knotting

Make cardboard or sandpaper patterns in the sizes given below. For each block, cut the indicated number of squares and triangles. Remember to leave a seam allowance outside the pencil line.

UNIT A (triangle made by cutting a 4" square diagonally in half; the sides of the triangle are therefore 4", 4", and $5\frac{3}{4}$".): Four blue, four white.

UNIT B (2" square): Ten blue, ten white.

FIGURE 46: The finished quilt top is pinned through the filler to the lining. Knots are made wherever there is a pin

FIGURE 47: Nine small blocks make up one large block

For the border, cut two strips 4″ x 37″ and two strips 4″ x 49″ from the blue fabric. Cut four 4″ squares of white fabric. This includes your ½″ seam allowances. The blocks can be pieced together either by hand or by machine, being careful to sew on the pencil outline.

Seam the squares into five four-patch blocks, and the triangles into four blue-and-white squares:

UNIT A   UNIT B

FIGURE 48: The small blocks

Arrange these nine small blocks into the Jacob's Ladder design as shown in the diagram. It is very helpful to have a 12″ cardboard square marked with the pattern to lay the pieces out on as you assemble and sew them. The most efficient way to assemble each block is to sew the short seams first, then the two long seams.

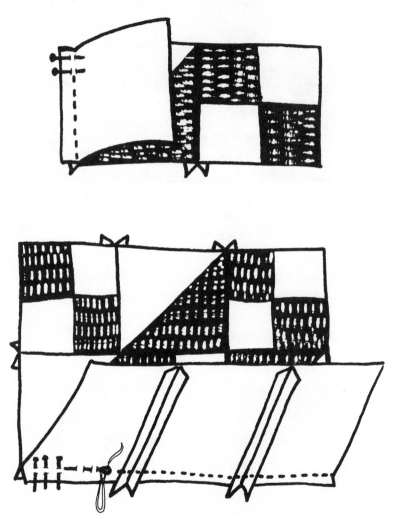

FIGURE 49: Putting together the blocks

When all twelve large blocks are assembled into one large piece, add the border. First sew the 37″ strips to the top side of the quilt at each end. Sew a white 4″ square to both ends of both 49″ strips, and sew these longer borders to the sides of the quilt top.

The lining is then laid out on a flat surface. Cotton fabrics now come wide enough so that it should be possible to find a fabric you can use for the lining without seaming, but seam it if necessary. Place the dacron filler on top of the lining material and spread the quilt top over everything, making a "sandwich." The lining material should extend 2″–3″ all around beyond the quilt top to allow for shifting while it is being knotted. Pin through all three thicknesses at 4″ intervals, taking care to keep all three layers smooth while you work. Knots are made using a double strand of pearl cotton wherever a pin has been placed. The decorative knot is made from the top of the quilt taking two horizontal stitches, or a cross stitch if a more decorative effect is desired, and tying a secure double knot (see Fig. 49), leaving ¾″ ends on the top of the quilt.

When all the knots are completed, trim excess dacron filling and lining material even, making certain to leave enough lining fabric to turn over to the right side of the quilt as a binding. Pin this carefully and stitch in place, using a blind stitch or a running stitch. Miter corners. If you prefer, packaged bias binding can be used.

"*JACOB'S LADDER*" TALLIT BAG

A *tallit* [prayer shawl] is put on in the morning by men and boys over thirteen, when there is enough light to see by. (It is also worn on Yom Kippur Eve, when it is put on before dark.) What constitutes enough light? According to one tradition, enough light enables one to distinguish between blue and green. This *tallit* bag was made in blue velvet and green wool, so the bag itself will be an aid in fulfilling the *mitzvah* [commandment] of the *tallit*.

FINISHED DIMENSIONS: 12″ square

MATERIALS:
¼ *yard blue velvet*
½ *yard green wool*
13″ x 25″ rectangle of lining fabric
12″ zipper, blue or green

FIGURE 50: *Tallit* bag using the same "Jacob's Ladder" pattern as the crib quilt

The unit sizes for the Jacob's Ladder block are given with the crib quilt. Use these to cut twenty green squares, twenty blue squares, eight blue triangles, and eight green triangles. This will give you two 12″-square Jacob's Ladder blocks (see Fig. 47). When the blocks are assembled, iron them. Before seaming together the two large squares you now have, attach the zipper to one side of each square, following directions on the zipper package. Fold the two squares so the right sides are facing one another, and seam the remaining three sides together. Fold the lining fabric in half, and sew both side seams.

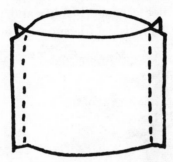

FIGURE 51: Lining for the *tallit* bag

Turn the lining pocket right side out and slide it over the *tallit* bag, which is still inside out. Fold the top seam allowance of the lining under, and slip-stitch the lining in place over the zipper-seam allowance of the *tallit* bag. Open zipper and turn right side out. If desired, make a tassel from threads pulled from the green wool and attach it to the zipper pull.

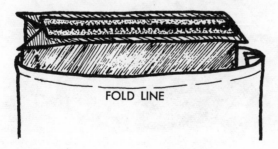

FOLD LINE

FIGURE 52: Inserting the lining, with zipper in place

STAR DOLL CARRIAGE QUILT

This miniature quilt was made for my daughter's favorite doll. It measures 18″ x 22″. I have made several of them as birthday gifts for her friends from leftover pieces of her dresses and from scraps given to me by the mothers of the little girls. By enlarging either the center panels or the borders, this quilt would make an attractive baby carriage quilt. A size of 24″ x 30″ makes a nice carriage blanket and is still not too big for dolls when the baby is a little more grown up.

FIGURE 53: Doll carriage with star quilt

Since this quilt was made from assorted leftover pieces, the measurements are quite irregular. Use whatever fabrics you have at hand, making certain that the front center panel is at least 12″ x 14″ to accommodate the star and that the back panel is large enough for the words *laylah tov* [goodnight] and roughly the same size as the front panel.

Quilt front:

1. Cut twelve triangles of equal size from assorted fabrics. The three sides of the triangle must all be of the same length.

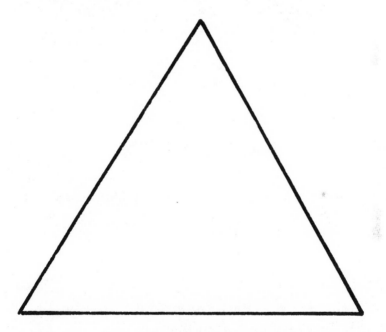

FIGURE 54: Pattern for triangle

2. Assemble star by first seaming pairs of triangles into diamond shapes and then sewing the diamonds together, starting from the center point each time. Turn under outer seam allowance; iron star.

FIGURE 55: The star assembled

3. Pin star to center of front panel and appliqué in place, using any decorative stitch you like. I used a feather stitch.
4. Attach border strips.

Quilt back:

Using the large cross stitch *alef-bet* in the Appendix (the letters in the photograph are a variation on it), draw the words *laylah tov*—or any other inscription or name you prefer—on a sheet of paper. Then transfer it onto the center back panel. Use dressmaker's tracing paper for this. Spray lightly with fixative. Cross-stitch in a contrasting color, using three strands of embroidery floss. Sew on border strips.

Spread the back of the quilt *face down* on a table. Place dacron quilt batting (or, if you have none left from a large project, use two layers of flannel, but it will not be as puffy) over this and put the quilt top over everything. Pin through all three thicknesses at 3″ intervals. Turn quilt over, and if the pins interfere with the letters, move them slightly. Make a knot at each pin, using six strands of the same embroidery floss used for the stitching. Leave ¾″ "tails" on the knots on the top of the quilt. When the knots are completed and the pins removed, trim all three layers even and finish the edge with packaged corded piping or bias binding.

FIGURE 56: The reverse side of the star quilt. The Hebrew words say *laylah tov* [goodnight]

TIE PATCHWORK TALLIT BAG

FINISHED DIMENSIONS: 10½″ x 13″ (closed)

MATERIALS AND SUPPLIES:

Fifteen years of outmoded ties, from which enough are selected to cut one hundred and ten triangles. Every family must still have a collection of once-favorite ties that are not worn out but which we cannot yet bring ourselves to discard. (The problem may someday be what to do with today's fashionable ties—or with all ties!) The ties I used were selected partially for their colors, but mainly for their nostalgic and

FIGURE 57: The patchwork *tallit* bag made of old neckties, showing inscription on the lining

emotional value. There are pieces from the tie my husband wore on our wedding day, a plaid tie he wore in college when we were dating, the tie we bought together on a trip to Portugal, that he never wore but we were attached to, a tie his brother gave him, and the black tie he wore for a month in mourning for President Kennedy. It's a pity that the *tallit* bag only uses about ten ties. Perhaps someday I'll get around to making a lap robe to take to football games from the rest of those hanging forlornly behind the closet door. For this pattern, half the fabric should be in dark tones and half in light.

lining fabric: 28" x 14"
embroidery thread
cardboard
1 package corded piping

1. Take the ties apart, discard the inner stiffening fabric. Iron ties open and flat.
2. Cut out of sandpaper or cardboard a triangle that is made by cutting a 2½" square in half along its diagonal.
3. Trace 55 light-colored triangles and 55 dark triangles on the fabrics. The drawn line is the sewing line, so it must be carefully done. Leave enough room between the triangles to allow for a ⅜" or ¼" seam allowance. Since ties are made of bias-cut fabric, care should be taken not to stretch the fabric while drawing the triangles.
4. Sew dark triangles to light along the diagonal seam. When you have 55 squares, iron them flat.
5. Arrange squares on a flat surface: 5 across and 11 down. By arranging the squares so that a dark triangle is always against a light triangle, an overall pinwheel effect is achieved.
6. Seam squares together in lines of five each. Then sew the long horizontal seams joining the rows of blocks. It is important to match the drawn seam line as much as possible in order to keep the squares lined up.

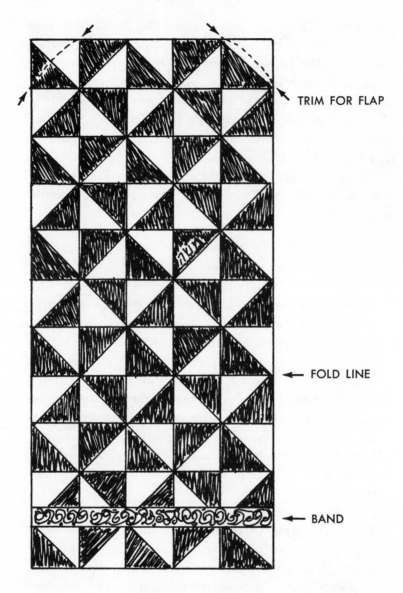

TRIM FOR FLAP

FOLD LINE

BAND

FIGURE 58: The arrangement of the squares for the *tallit* bag

7. Decide which end will be the flap, and trim it into a slight curve.

8. Embroider the name or initials of the recipient anywhere, as you desire. Cut the lining fabric to match the curve of the flap and embroider a suitable inscription or name on it. Chain, outline, cross, or running stitch seem to me most compatible with patchwork.

9. For the band: cut a piece of tie 13½″ by 3″, fold in half lengthwise (right sides out), and sew the sides together. Turn inside out and iron with the seam centered on one side of the band. Sew band to the seam line at either side of the end of the rectangle (not the flap end), centering it over the seam between the first two rows of squares.

10. Stitch the corded piping to the seam allowance all around the bag, including the band you have just attached.

11. Fold the rectangle, right sides together, along the seam four rows from the straight end. Seam both sides. Do the same with the lining fabric.

12. Slide the lining into place and slip-stitch around edge of flap and opening.

A patchwork project for table linens is discussed on pp. 148–56.

Needlepoint

WITH NEEDLEPOINT, as with the other techniques in this book, I would recommend a sampler if you have never done this type of embroidery before. In this case, however, the sampler cannot be included in the patchwork assemblage (Fig. 9), because its heaviness in comparison to the other fabrics would destroy the overall effect. On the sampler you can master the basic needlepoint stitches and learn to work so as to cause minimal distortion of the canvas, thereby making the blocking operation at the end an easy chore.

As a sampler I would recommend one simple shape on a solid background, to be used as either a pincushion, small framed piece, key case, or a pocket for a pair of jeans. The musical instrument designs or the fish are suitable for this learning project. Rather than investing in the more expensive needlepoint yarns or the very expensive "Persian" wool, play with multicolored yarn from the five-and-ten-cent store. The multicolored yarn hides mistakes, so you don't have to rip anything out in order to "get it right." It is amusing to use, because it produces a design with no effort on your part, and you can practice changing direction, stitch, and color without fear that you have done something wrong. The design evolves as you sew. The fish's striations are limited only by the basic fish outline and your imagination. Cut the yarn at any point when you decide either to change color or to have more of the same.

FISH PINCUSHION

The fish is an ancient and universal symbol of fertility and abundance. It has been used extensively as a decorative motif in Jewish art. The fish is the emblem of the tribe of Ephraim. It is especially popular for use on Purim decorations since the fish is the zodiac symbol for the month of Adar (February–March) when Purim—the joyous holiday commemorating the rescue of Persian Jewry by the beautiful Queen Esther and her cousin Mordecai from the evil plans of Haman—takes place. The Hebrew letters for the month of Adar אדר could be added to make this as a gift for someone whose birthday falls then or whose name is Esther or Mordecai.

Fish is an important part of Sabbath and holiday meals, and it is the rare festive gathering that doesn't include in its menu a dish of gefilte fish or herring in some form. This culinary predilection probably owes some of its popularity to the association of fish with the primeval sea monster, the Leviathan, upon which, according to talmudic legend, the righteous will feast when the Messiah comes. Since the pleasures of the Sabbath are considered to be one-sixtieth of the pleasures of Paradise, the traditional fish course becomes a symbolic foretaste of the world to come.

To make the 5″ x 9″ oval pincushion, you will need a piece of canvas that is 9″ x 13″. Needlepoint canvas is usually made of cotton but sometimes of linen. It is woven to form a regular grid pattern of squares. It is available with as few as three squares to the running inch (which is used for rug-making) and as many as forty squares to the inch. The latter is so fine that it is almost like fabric. The most commonly used mesh size is No. 10; that is, canvas with ten squares to the inch. When finer details and more graceful curves are desired, a higher-number mesh is chosen. The type of canvas used for the projects in this book is called "mono" or single-thread canvas.

FIGURE 59: Fish pincushion

("Penelope" canvas is woven with two threads forming each mesh, thereby making it possible to divide the square and double the number of stitches per inch on a section of the canvas when more detail is desired.)

For No. 10 canvas, a size 18 tapestry needle is usually the most comfortable, but for use with worsted yarn rather than needlepoint yarn you might want to use a lower number, which is slightly larger. Tapestry needles have large eyes and blunt points. They come in sizes ranging from 13 to 24. The higher-number needles are used on the finer, higher-number canvases.

Tape the edges of the canvas with masking or adhesive tape to prevent it from raveling or snagging the wool. Enlarge the fish outline and draw it on the canvas, using an indelible felt-tip pen.

FIGURE 60: Design for the fish pincushion, with grid

Though all of the tent stitches appear the same when worked, the most important one is the basketweave, which produces a characteristic woven effect on the back of the work. This stitch causes the least amount of distortion of the canvas and, though it uses the largest quantity of yarn, is the most durable, and, I find, most pleasant to do. Wherever the pattern makes it impossible to use the basketweave stitch, fill in with a continental or a half-cross stitch (that is, half of the cross stitch used for embroidery, Fig. 23), but try to use as much basketweave as possible.

Thread your needle with yarn approximately 18″ long. Start your stitches at the upper right of the fish's body, before the curve of the tail. This will give you a wide space to practice the basketweave stitch, until you feel ready to undertake the tail. The basketweave stitch is made in diagonal rows. By stopping and changing direction when you come to the felt-tipped line, the outline of the fish takes shape. I prefer this to working the outline first, which tends to produce an unattractive ridge around the outside of the shape. When the fish is complete, reembroider the eye with six or eight lazy daisy stitches. Fill in the background. Block and trim according to the directions below.

The pincushion was finished by making a backing the same size as the embroidered canvas from a piece of heavy cotton twill. The backing was placed face down on the needlepoint and the two seamed together by machine, leaving a small opening to allow it to be turned right side out. The little "pillow case" thus made was then stuffed tightly with cotton balls. Using nine strands of the same yarn that I had used for the needlepoint, I made a long braid which was then slip-stitched in place along the same line and a bow tied on top.

TO BLOCK NEEDLEPOINT

If you have used the basketweave stitch, a minimum of distortion will have occurred and blocking will be easier. You will need a flat, porous surface to block the embroidery on. A piece of plywood, drawing board, or the back of a door where the holes won't matter will do nicely.

Draw the measurements of your embroidery on a large sheet of paper, indicating the center line in both directions. Tape this in place on your board.

Place the needlepoint face down on the blocking paper. Using a sponge and cold water, thoroughly dampen the work; it should be damp but not dripping. A little vinegar in the water prevents the colors from running.

Using a staple gun (these can be rented or borrowed from most hardware stores and some fabric stores, or your local kindergarten might have one which they use for decorating bulletin boards), staple the needlepoint to the board through the paper. Place the first staples on the center lines about ½″ outside of the last row of stitches. Do not staple through the needlework itself. With the next four staples, secure the corners of the piece against the board in their proper position. To your horror the embroidery will seem hopelessly warped, but by gentle tugging and stapling, the work will soon lie flat. The canvas alone is strong, and worked as it is with wool it is sturdier yet, so do not be afraid to pull hard in order to stretch it into shape. Keep stapling until there is no more give in the piece. That may mean two or three rows of staples.

Dampen again and allow to dry thoroughly. This usually takes two to four days. It is better to leave it on the stretching board until you are absolutely certain that it is thoroughly dry than to run the risk of its warping again. Most needlepoint authorities tell you to use rustproof upholstery tacks and to do the stretching with hammer and nails, but I much prefer the staple gun for its speed and efficiency, and I cannot see that it makes any difference in the final result. The staples will hold the needlepoint every bit as securely as nails or tacks.

When the work is thoroughly dry, remove the staples with a screwdriver. To prevent unraveling after the tape is removed: With a sewing machine, sew two wavy lines close to the needlepoint all around on the unworked canvas. Or apply glue (Elmer's works well) all around, in the same place you would sew.

Trim away excess canvas. If your work is a pillow, pincushion, or belt, you will only need ½" all around as a seam allowance. For a framed piece, leave 2½" to 3", turn under ½" hem, and stitch.

Many people are afraid to block and mount their own needlepoint projects. Think of the completed needlepoint as if it were a heavyweight upholstery fabric. If you feel up to handling the dressmaking details in ordinary fabric, you could probably do it with needlepointed fabric. Needlepoint pillows, pincushions, simple purses or bags, pockets, belts, and even some upholstery projects, to mention just a few, can be done at home. I would leave luggage or other things with elaborate construction or hardware to experts. Usually the place where you purchase your needlework equipment can give you the address of a professional needlepoint mounter if you need one.

When you are ready to undertake a more ambitious project, you will probably want to use a better-quality yarn. Many different yarns are available for needlepoint, and it is entirely possible to use even those yarns not specifically made for this technique. One can introduce cotton pearl, or even silk threads when special effects are desired. For the canvas projects in this book, I have used either what is called tapestry yarn, Persian wool, or crewel yarn, because these are almost universally available. The only exception is the fish pincushion, which was worked in ordinary knitting worsted from the five-and-ten-cent store. The important characteristic of needlepoint and Persian yarns is that they have especially long fibers. This means that they are very long wearing and extremely pleasant to work with since they do not become worn and frazzled while being drawn through the canvas, which knitting yarn tends to do. Persian yarn is twice as expensive as the ordinary needlepoint yarn but has a lovely luster and comes in an incredible range of hues. (For all but the largest projects, however, the extra cost is only a few dollars.) The blues, reds, and purples are especially nice, while the earth tones are quite satisfactory in the less expensive yarn.

Yarn is usually sold by the ounce; but in some localities it is possible to buy it by the strand. For those colors where just a small amount is necessary, I have indicated the number of feet of the color required. If you can, just buy that amount; if not, you will have some left over for your next project.

GUITAR STRAPS

> Sing unto the Lord; for He hath done gloriously.
>
> Isaiah 12:5

The ancient Mediterranean world abounded with deities that could be and were visualized. While other gods and goddesses made themselves available to their devotees through visual manifestations (statues, carvings, and paintings), the Hebrew God chose to communicate with His people through the auditory phenomenon of a disembodied Voice. On occasion, the Voice emerged from a physical object such as a burning bush, but it was understood that this was for "appearances only" and did not constitute the permanent form of God. The prime vehicle of communication between the Jew and God was the ear rather than the eye. Perhaps this in part explains the intense involvement Jews have always had with music. The Torah is traditionally chanted rather than read. Melody enhances and facilitates learning.

FIGURE 61: Needlepoint guitar straps

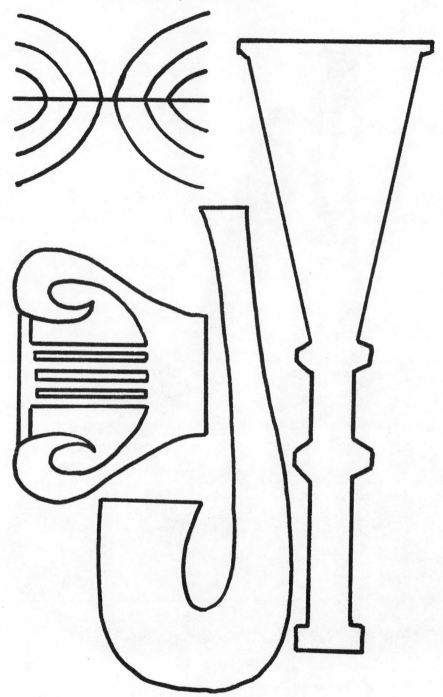

FIGURE 62: Patterns for the musical instruments

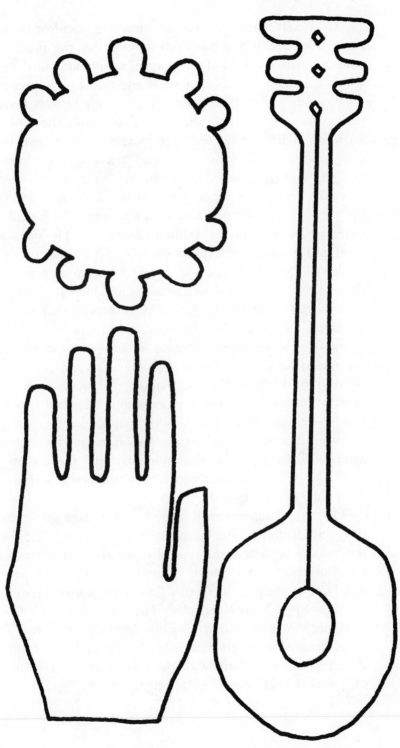

An Israeli friend related an amusing incident that took place when she was a law student. One day the professor announced that every student in turn would be called upon to read a section of the Talmud aloud and then to interpret it. One young man had terrible difficulty. Though he was known to be very capable and read the ancient text easily, he could make no sense of it whatsoever. Then, totally embarrassed, he confessed to the class that since he had had a very Orthodox upbringing and had learned to study by chanting, the only way he could understand the text would be to chant it. He put on his *yarmulka*, stood up, and began to sway back and forth, chanting the text in the traditional manner. He then gave a lucid and profound interpretation of what he had read.

Jewish "style" in music, as in art, has taken on many colorations from the different environments in which Jews have lived. In turn, the music of the Jews has influenced that of the host countries. For example, although many writers on flamenco ignore its Jewish origins, stressing only its Moorish ones, others say that at least the *petenera* and *tango-flamenco* styles are derived from Hebrew liturgical music. Through song we can express thoughts and emotions we might be afraid to admit to otherwise. The tribulations of the Spanish Jews in the period of the Inquisition found expression in what seem to be romantic ballads. Like the Marranos who sang them, these songs (many of which are still current in flamenco repertoires) say more than at first appears.

Of the instruments used as designs for these guitar straps—lyre, lute, trumpet, tambourine, and *shofar* [ram's horn]—only the last can be considered typically Jewish. The others, including those that were used in Temple worship—trumpet, harp, and lyre, as well as shepherd's flute (not shown here)—originated among Oriental peoples. The triumphal arch of Titus in Rome shows the Roman legions carrying away the Temple instruments along with their other booty. A hand is shown on the strap because, along with the human voice, it is the oldest of "musical instruments" (clapping).

Since both my sons play the guitar, I couldn't very well make only one guitar strap. The boys picked the colors. One strap was made with light forms (yellow) on a dark background (brown), and the other with dark forms (purple) on a white background. The effect of each is quite different. It is also possible to sew each instrument in a different color, or to have a third color for the *menorot* which are used to space the instruments.

FINISHED SIZE: $2\frac{1}{4}$" x 52"

MATERIALS:

6" of 54" wide cotton mono No. 10 canvas
yarn: $2\frac{1}{2}$ ounces of background color; 2 ounces for the instruments
commercial guitar strap for hardware and lining if desired

Tape together pieces of graph paper to measure 54" long and 3" wide. Arrange instruments to suit yourself, beginning and ending with a trumpet facing in opposite directions. Draw *menorah* forms as spacers between the instruments.

With masking tape, secure the drawing to a large work surface. If you do not have a table that is long enough, use the floor. Place the canvas over the drawing. Select a thread 2" in along the long edge of the canvas as the top edge of your strap. Carefully mark this thread with an indelible felt-tip pen. Line up the inked thread along the top edge of your drawing.

Tape the canvas in place over the drawing. If the drawing is dark enough it will show through the canvas mesh and you can trace it onto the canvas. It isn't necessary to color in the forms; outlines do just as well.

The entire strap is worked in basketweave tent stitch. Add one row of continental stitch along what will be the fold lines at the long sides of the strap. Do this row in the darkest color you are using. With something of such peculiar dimensions, it is especially important to use the basketweave stitch, because the continental stitch could make the strap turn into a corkscrew. There was such minimal distortion that I was tempted not to block the finished strap at all, and only did in order to be consistent.

Blocking something so long presents a problem unless you have a wall, door, or bookshelf that you do not mind mutilating. I stapled the straps to my studio wall, which is plywood.

After the strap has been blocked and trimmed, you can complete it with lining and hardware cannibalized from a commercial guitar strap or by lining it with grosgrain ribbon or iron-on tape and making buttonholes at each end or attaching loops. Because my sons wanted the straps to be adjustable and strong, I used the buckles and leather end-pieces from inexpensive guitar straps. Do not take apart the strap until you are ready to add your own needlepoint so that its construction will be fresh in your mind. I did not use the lining, which was plastic, but instead used a heavy strip of canvas for the backing. I assembled the strap and, with paper clips, held the leather end-pieces in place. The local shoemaker sewed them to the needlepoint using his heavy-duty machine.

If you do use a commercial guitar strap as a base, get a strap that is sewn, not riveted, through the leather. However, it doesn't matter if the buckle end is riveted, because that can be simply cut away and discarded and the buckle sewn to your work by the shoemaker. But the leather end-piece must not be riveted.

THE LION AND THE DOVE TALLIT BAG

The lion is an ancient Jewish symbol of political, military, and spiritual strength. It is mentioned in the Bible more than any other undomesticated animal. It is the ensign of the Tribe of Judah and was used by King Solomon as a decorative motif on the throne and the huge brass washbasin of the Temple. The lion is the fifth sign of the zodiac, corresponding to the mouth of Ab (אב) in the lunar Hebrew calendar and roughly

FIGURE 63: The Lion and the Dove *tallit* bag

to the July–August period in the common calendar. After the destruction of the Temple, the lion became a standard motif in synagogue decoration. Pairs of lions often served to support the Ark of the Law or the tablets of the Ten Commandments placed on top of the Ark. They have been worked in silver as Torah crowns and breastplates, embroidered on Torah mantles and Ark curtains, carved on Ark doors, and set into mosaic floors and murals. Many family and first names in Hebrew and other languages are derived from the word "lion": Leo, Leon, Lionel, Leonard, Leib, Lowe, Loewy, Lyon, Ari, Aryeh.

The lion has become almost a cliché as a decorative motif, and lately has gone out of fashion and is little used by serious contemporary designers. Still, I think there is a lot of emotional mileage left in the old lion. Perhaps we need fresh interpretations rather than a new symbol. Here is a friendly lion in gay colors hosting a dove on his tail. His strength is still apparent in silhouette; though still King of Beasts, he can coexist with the dove. The banner carried by the lion bears the inscription "strong as a lion" because one should be "strong as a lion, to do the will of thy Father who is in heaven" (Pirke Abot ["Sayings of the Fathers"] V, 23). What the world needs now is a benevolent lion.

This *tallit* bag was worked with No. 14 mono canvas because I wanted the checkerboard effect to be small in scale and the curves well defined. It could be done on No. 10 or No. 12 canvas for a bolder effect. The body could be worked in stripes of different-color basketweave stitch rather than the checkerboard. It would also be very striking if the entire design—grass, banner, bird, and lion—were all done in the same color against a contrasting background. In that case it would resemble the paper-cut upon which its design was based (Fig. 6). The design was made as a *tallit* bag but could easily be adapted for use as a cushion cover or wall ornament. The pattern is here reduced to half its size, but it could be enlarged more than twice for a large hanging on No. 10 canvas.

The finished *tallit* bag is 10″ x 12″. You will therefore need a piece of canvas that is at least 14″ x 16″. If you make a needlepoint back for the bag as well, you will need another piece of canvas the same size. While the reverse could be a piece of heavy velvet, wool, or silk in a color to match one of those used in the embroidery, the back of this *tallit* bag is also done in needlepoint. The background color is the same as that of the lion, and a border of the checkerboard stitch forms an open rectangle 1″ in from the edge.

Tape the edges of the canvas with masking tape. Enlarge the drawing of the Lion and the Dove either photographically

EACH SQUARE = 1"

FIGURE 64: Pattern for the Lion and the Dove *tallit* bag, with grid

or by the grid method. Place the drawing on a table and the canvas over it. You will be able to see the drawing through the canvas. Using the drawing as a guide, draw the design on the canvas with acrylic paints or indelible felt-tip pens. It is not necessary to detail the checkerboard on the canvas; that is better done by counting it out as you go. Once the first 1″ unit is done, the rest follow easily.

YARN AND STITCHES:
Background: wine red 4 oz.; basketweave tent stitch.
Bird: white ½ oz.; eye: wine red; legs: yellow; upright cross stitch.
Banner and grass: olive green ½ oz.; basketweave tent stitch.
Letters: turquoise ¼ oz.; tent stitch. The turquoise was also used as the center tent stitch in the checkerboard pattern on the lion's body.
Lion: turquoise as indicated above, yellow 1½ oz., pink 1½ oz., orange 1½ oz. The lion's mane was worked in yellow, using an upright cross stitch to differentiate it from the yellow face, which was worked in a basketweave tent stitch. The body and tail were done in a checkerboard stitch.

By studying the diagrams in the stitch section (Figs. 40, 42) and the detail photograph (Fig. 39) there, you will see that the checkerboard is made up of alternating squares of Scotch stitch and tent stitch. By using two colors (pink and orange) for the Scotch stitch and two (gold and turquoise) for the tent stitch, the checkerboard seems far more complicated than it really is.

After the needlepoint is finished and blocked, seam the front and back together by machine along the bottom and both sides. Use the last row of needlepoint stitches as a guide for your seam line; this way no bare canvas will show. Make a silk lining according to the directions with the "Jacob's Ladder" *tallit* bag (p. 77), and insert a zipper by hand at the top. Use nine strands of yarn (in the background color) to make a braid, and sew it over the seam line if you desire.

Yarmulkas

MATCHING *yarmulkas* [skullcaps] were crocheted from the yarn left over from the needlepoint guitar straps. They are shown here with a group of *yarmulkas* made as gifts for various occasions.

The smallest *yarmulka* was made for the *brit* [circumcision ceremony] of the son of some friends of ours. It was made by folding tiny darts in a circle of white cotton fabric. The darts were then embroidered to hold them in place, and tiny ties of soutache braid were added to keep the *yarmulka* on the baby. I have made these as gifts for a number of friends, and everyone seems to like them because they make a very sentimental memento.

Using a standard commercial *yarmulka* as the pattern and, ultimately, as the lining, a wool and velvet *yarmulka* was made to match the green and blue "Jacob's Ladder" *tallit* bag. It would also be fun to make a *yarmulka* using pieces of old ties. After the seams are done, they could be reembroidered in the manner of a Victorian crazy quilt.

The largest of the *yarmulkas* was constructed in the manner of the hats worn by the Druse of Israel. Druse hats are brightly embroidered on white fabric. This one is more formal, made of deep red velour embroidered in black and gold pearl cotton.

Wearing a headcovering is a comparatively recent phenomenon in Jewish history. It is not mentioned in the Torah;

FIGURE 65: Five *yarmulkas;* the Druse-style *yarmulka* is at the center, rear

neither is it required by talmudic law. The custom was probably adopted by the Jews in Babylonia in imitation of the local population, which wore headcoverings both as protection from the sun and as a matter of courtesy. In most of the Western world, respect is shown by removing one's hat. In most of the Eastern world, however, courtesy demands that you remove your shoes and cover your head.

Many Jews emigrated from Babylonia when that country's economic and cultural life went into a decline in the eighth century. Many of them settled in Spain and brought the custom of wearing a pointed Persian hat with them. Since the Moslems who then ruled Spain wore turbans, the Jews retained the Babylonian-style hat to maintain their separateness. Wearing a headcovering became a firmly established custom among the Jews of Spain. It was not at all common in the rest of Europe until the Expulsion of Spanish Jewry by *los Reyes Catolicos* (the Catholic Monarchs), Ferdinand and Isabella, in 1492, when the fleeing Jews spread the custom to other Jewish communities to the north and east, where it still was not universally practiced until about the eighteenth century. In the nineteenth century the Reform movement, coming full circle, tried to abolish the use of a headcovering by saying that it was not ordained in the Torah.

But a custom once established is difficult to uproot, and what began as a health measure and sign of good manners was reinterpreted and justified in spiritual terms. Looking into the past is a little like Freudian analysis: it may reveal the basic roots of a situation, but it does not necessarily change anything. Since slaves in ancient days kept their heads covered as a sign of servitude, the Jewish headcovering may also symbolize humility and service to God. While expressing humility and awe in relation to the Divine Presence, the *yarmulka* is also a mark of distinction, since it immediately identifies the Jew both to his fellow Jews and to strangers.

To make this Druse-style *yarmulka*, cut a strip of velour which is 22" long and 5" wide. Also cut a 3" velour circle. Since velour stretches and curls, the most difficult part of working with it is making certain to cut it accurately. Cut pieces with the same measurements from lining fabric. The best lining fabric is cotton batiste lining, which stabilizes the velour without adding too much bulk.

Seam the two ends of the velour strip, forming a crown. Do the same with the lining strip.

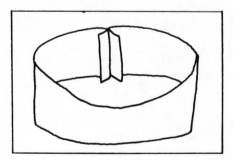

FIGURE 66: Crown for the *yarmulka*

Pin the lining to the velour crown, wrong sides together. Turn in ¼″ seam allowance at the top and bottom and blind-stitch the two parts together. Line the 3″ circle in the same manner. Using a large running stitch, gather the top of the crown until it just fits around the disk of lined velour. Blind-stitch the gathered crown to the edge of the disk.

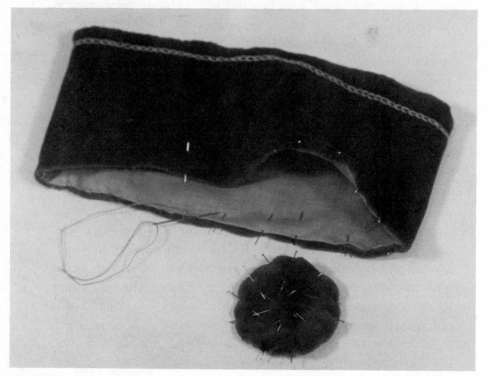

FIGURE 67: The two sections of the *yarmulka* have been lined, and some of the embroidery is completed

The embroidery, which is made up of simple rows of chain stitch and threaded running stitch using heavy-weight No. 5 pearl cotton, can be done before or after the *yarmulka* is assembled.

Dolls

THE FIRST DOLL I can remember making was done in the first grade. The body was constructed from the wire used to hold the paper caps on milk bottles. The head was a ball of absorbent cotton covered with pink crepe paper, strips of which were also wound around the wire limbs. Since that time I have loved to make dolls. Unlike commercially manufactured dolls, the ones we make take on some of our own personality even if we don't intend them to.

Possibilities for Jewish dolls might include biblical dolls (imagine a Jonah-in-the-whale doll—a zipper-mouth whale containing a removable Jonah), our own version of traditional or contemporary character dolls found in gift shops, and holiday dolls (perhaps a miniature *sukkah* with a doll family to enjoy it).

Since children (and most adults) are intrigued with twins, exclaiming over the double-yolked egg or the cherries that grow two to the stem, not to mention human twins, I decided to do a twin doll. Although my doll is modeled after a sign of the zodiac, the pair could be dressed differently as Jacob and Esau, David and Jonathan, or Ruth and Naomi.

MAZZAL TOV *DOLL*

Almost everyone is familiar with the congratulatory expression *mazzal tov*, which is commonly translated as "good luck." The dictionary meaning of *mazzal* however, is "constellation,

FIGURE 68: The *Mazzal Tov* doll

planet; destiny, fate." *Tov* means "good." When we wish someone *mazzal tov*, either in recognition of an achievement or as a
wish for success in a forthcoming undertaking, we are making
an astrological association between human fate and the stars.

Several other words derived from the Hebrew root *mazzal*
are also worth discussing. The word *shlimazal* describes that
unfortunate for whom everything is a disaster (another word
with an astrological origin). No wonder: he is under a negative
constellation. The Sephardic Jews have two expressions that are
also based on the word *mazzal*: in Ladino (the medieval Spanish
mixed with Hebrew spoken by descendants of those Jews who
were driven out of Spain by the Inquisition and Expulsion),
someone who is *desmazalado* is a "poor thing" like the *shlimazal*;
in modern Spanish dictionaries, *desmazalado* is translated as
"weak, dejected, fainthearted, spiritless." Speakers of Ladino
also use the expression *mazzal alto* [a high constellation] to wish
one another good luck and congratulations, while *mazzal tov* is
used with less frequency.

The zodiac [*mazzalot* in Hebrew] probably developed as a
device for measuring time. Its divisions are better suited to the
Hebrew calendar, which is lunar, than to the calendar in common usage. The twelve zodiac signs correspond accurately to
each Hebrew month, instead of overlapping as they do in the
ordinary calendar.

While the cruder forms of star worship were forbidden,
Jewish mystics saw a parallel between higher and lower planes.
They felt that the smallest blade of grass on earth had its spe-
cially appointed star in heaven. The relationship between
heaven and earth was seen to be not one of cause and effect
but rather of correspondence; whatever happened in one
sphere had a mirror image in the other sphere.

Rabbinic Judaism, on the other hand, has always felt that
astrology is a delusion. In Jeremiah 10:2 there is the admonition:
"Learn not the ways of the nations, and be not dismayed at the
signs of heaven." But in spite of this injunction, the zodiac and
astrological motifs have been used as decoration on mosaic

synagogue floors, wedding contracts, and prayerbooks as well
as on calendars.

This doll is modeled after the interpretation of the zodiac
symbol for the month of Sivan (May–June), depicted in the
mosaic floor of the sixth-century Bet Alpha synagogue in the
Valley of Jezreel, Israel. The Hebrew names of the zodiac
figures are translations of the Latin names. The "Gemini" symbol of the twins is called *Teomim* in Hebrew. King David was
a Gemini–*Teomim*. (I tell you this so as to be in step with
newspaper horoscopes which always indicate famous people
born under the various signs.)

FINISHED SIZE: 24″ high

MATERIALS:

½ *yard print fabric*
1 yard matching solid color for face and limbs
30 oz. 4-ply knitting yarn (synthetic)
24 oz. polyester fiber filling
scrap fabric for shoes
cotton pearl or embroidery thread for features
packaged corded piping: cut two pieces 37½″ long and
16½″ long
star-shaped buttons or other ornaments if desired

Body: Cut two rectangles 16½″ x 10½″; this allows ¼″
seam allowance. Cut a strip 12½″ x 6″; cut this in half the long
way and trim the corners to oval shape; this will make the
base panel.

Limbs and Heads: Make cardboard patterns for the limbs
and head. Fold solid-color fabric in half, right sides together,
and draw around the cardboard patterns onto the fabric with
a sharp pencil. Draw the head twice, and the arms and legs
each four times. For shoes, use the bottom part of the leg
pattern. The drawn line will be the sewing line. Pin the folded
fabric together along this line and then cut out, leaving ¼″
seam allowances.

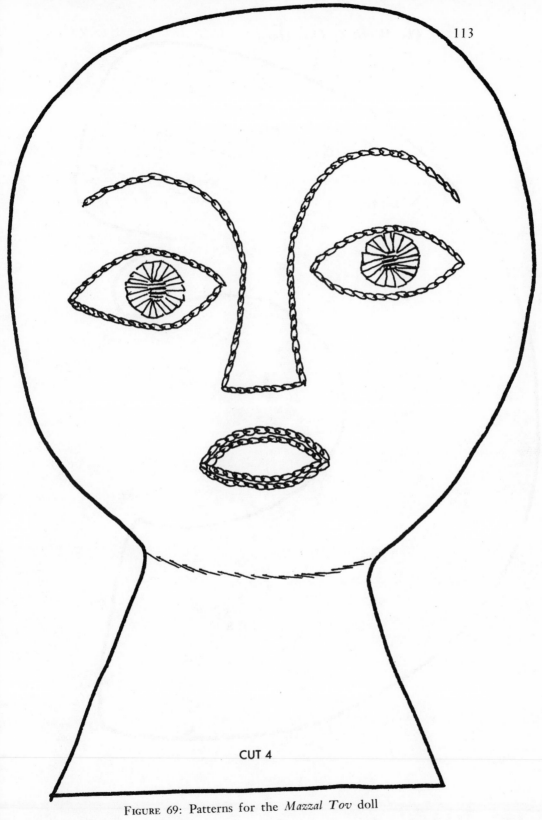

CUT 4

FIGURE 69: Patterns for the *Mazzal Tov* doll

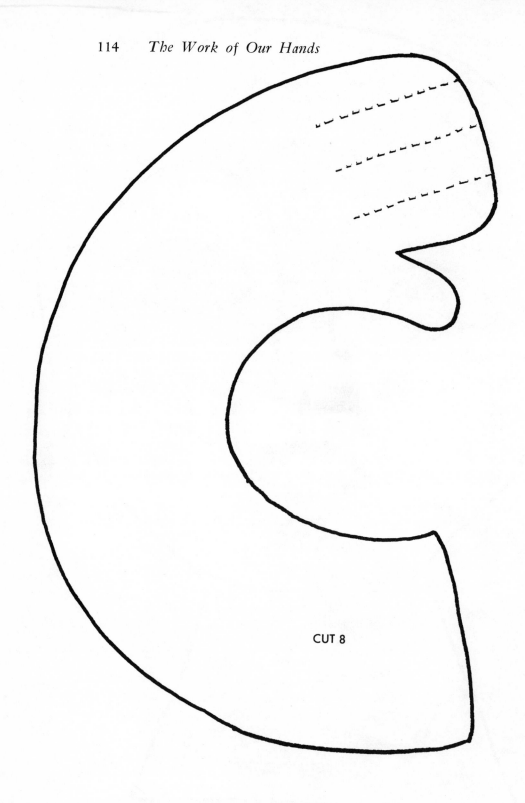

CUT 8

CUT 8

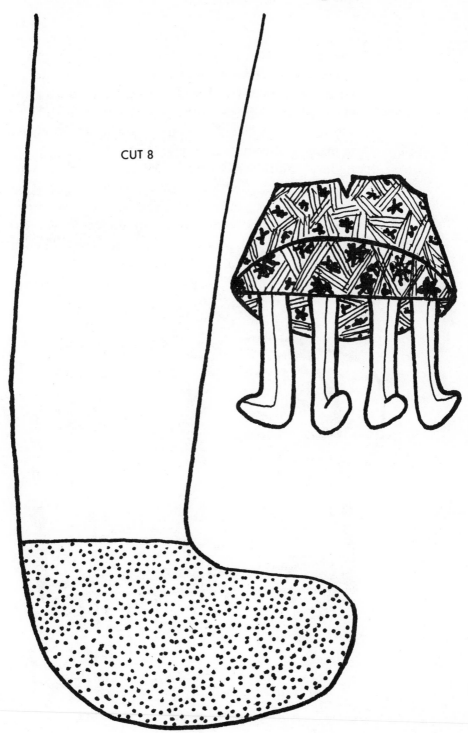

Assembly:

1. Sew around all limbs twice (for strong seams), leaving one end open. Clip at the curves. Turn right side out. Stuff legs compactly. Using a zipper foot on the machine (if you are sewing by machine), stitch the open end of the legs closed. If you are sewing by hand, sew as close to the stuffing as you can.

2. Lightly stuff hands, then sew on indicated lines (through the stuffed hand) to define the fingers. Continue to stuff the arms. Stitch the open ends closed.

3. Pin legs into the center seam allowance of the two halves of the base panel and stitch in place. The legs

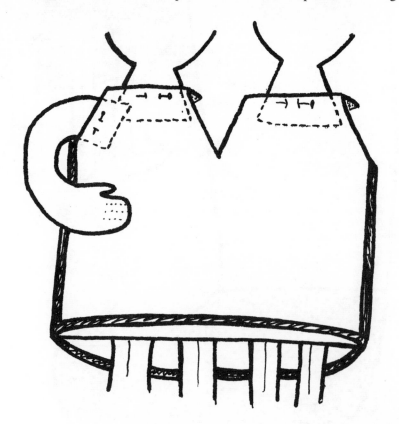

FIGURE 70: Attaching the arms and heads

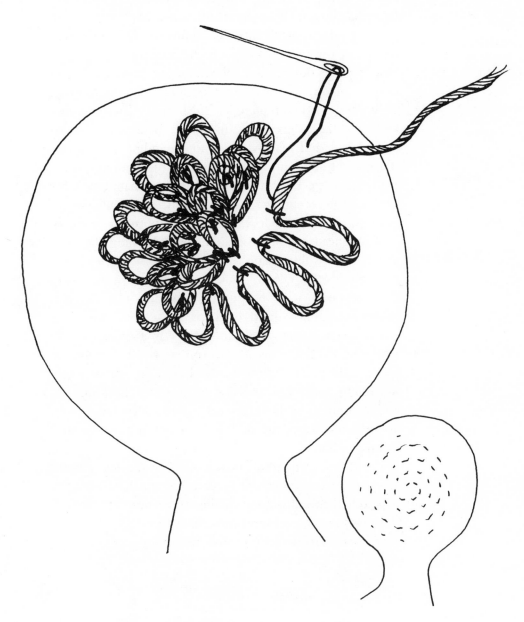

FIGURE 71: Attaching the hair

can be arranged in any way to suit your fancy—facing front as shown, or some front, some side, some back.

4. Cut a 2″-deep notch into the center of the body rectangles at the top, and clip off the corners.

5. Sew piping along seam allowance of both sides and bottom of one of the rectangles, and along the bottom only of the other rectangle. Turn right sides together and sew the side seams. Insert the base with the attached legs and seam all around, including the piping. Turn right side out and stuff up to the armpits.

6. Embroider the faces as shown. I used a chain stitch for everything except the pupils of the eyes, which are satin stitch, and the irises, which are buttonhole stitch. Sew the head and stuff it compactly, keeping the neck as long as possible. Seam the bottom of the neck closed.

7. Starting at the center back, loop the yarn hair and tack in place with heavy-duty thread. The diagram shows only one strand of yarn for clarity, but it is much faster if you do four strands at a time.

8. Insert heads and arms at the top of the body; pin in place. Add more stuffing to the body. Sew front seam, beginning under one arm and crossing the neckline and ending under the farthest arm. Insert as much stuffing as you can to get the doll as compact as possible, and finish sewing.

9. Make shoes, using the bottom half of the leg pattern as your pattern. Since the shoes are so small, it is simpler to stitch them all *before* cutting them out. Blind-stitch the shoes in place around the ankles.

10. Add star buttons around the neckline.

Table Linens

SINCE THE DESTRUCTION of the Temple in Jerusalem by the Romans in the year 70 C.E., the home table has become the altar for the Jewish family. Holidays such as Pesah, Shavuot, and Sukkot, which were originally festivals on which pilgrimages to the Temple and sacrifices were made, became home celebrations for the Jews in exile. The Sabbath, even though it occurs weekly, is generally regarded as the most important of Jewish holidays, and is characterized by family gatherings around the table. Every family develops its own "style" and its own Sabbath foods, but a universal ingredient is the willingness to put aside the weekday world and to assume what the Talmud calls the special soul God gives us on Sabbath eve and which departs again at the end of the Sabbath. The Sabbath exists so that work will not overwhelm and crush us. By varying our usual pattern one day a week, we are freed from enslavement to endless routine. The Sabbath is a time for study and for filling the mind with exalted thoughts and ideas. This has been especially important to the poor who, without a prescribed day of rejuvenation, might be forced to work ceaselessly and never have opportunities for ennobling thought and reflection. On the Sabbath, every man is a king, every woman a queen. Because of this spiritual transformation, it is often said that "more than the Jew has kept the Sabbath, the Sabbath has kept the Jew."

Our table in the kitchen in apartment 11 at 854 East 175 Street was a heavy wooden affair with a complicated understructure where my sister and I had innumerable battles for the most comfortable niches for our feet. The top was brownenameled metal, grained somehow to look like wood. Of course it didn't, but no one is fooled by Formica nowadays either. I knew almost every swirl in that table top. Because it could be sponged off and kept immaculate, our plates were placed directly on it; placemats, like top sheets, were cultural manifestations I did not learn about until years later. I also did my homework at that table.

On Thursday night, after everyone else was in bed and before she went to sleep, my mother would wash the kitchen floor—that was always the first sign of the transformation. By the time I came home from school on Friday afternoon the apartment was full of wonderful smells and my mother had either just bathed or was about to. So I would go to buy the *hallah*. My mother gave me the last coins she had saved from my father's yellow weekly pay envelope. Rarely would there still be a whole dollar left. If there was a little extra, I could buy peanuts or gum from the machine outside the bakery. The money always smelled of putty. Sometimes there even was putty caught in the bas relief of Lincoln's face. My father was a glazier, and everything about him smelled of putty when I was a child. It was an honest, pleasant smell. It meant there was work and then my parents wouldn't look so worried. Sometimes my mother gave me only enough money for half a *hallah* ("we wouldn't finish a whole one anyway").

By the time I came back with the *hallah*, the kitchen transformation was complete. The prosaic homework table was covered with a stiffly starched and ironed tablecloth, and Shabbat was almost here.

ROUND SHABBAT HALLAH *COVER AND MINIATURE*

The design for this *hallah* cover was derived, as has already been mentioned in the Design section, from a woodcut illustration in a seventeenth-century book of customs (see p. 18). Many such books were printed. They developed from series of individual sheets which were instructions for the proper observation of various holidays. For us they are a record of the manner in which the customs we practice today were observed by Jews in other places and times.

In the illustration here, the Sabbath lights are being kindled in an oil lamp suspended from the ceiling. Such lamps were

FIGURE 72: Round Shabbat *hallah* cover, with miniature

common throughout Europe. They were raised against the ceiling during the week and lowered for the Sabbath and lit before nightfall on Friday evening.

The origins of the custom of beginning Jewish holidays in the evening are obscure. The same biblical phrases are often quoted in making contradictory points about it. I like to think that Jewish holidays begin at night as a sign of faith. The idea that the day begins in the evening, when everything is slipping into darkness, rather than with the strident rays of the rising sun, is very much in keeping with the concept of an invisible but omnipresent God.

FINISHED SIZE: 16″ circle

MATERIALS:
½ yard of linen-weave fabric, heavy muslin, crash, or anything with a homespun texture is suitable
six-strand embroidery floss: dark brown, medium brown, or rust; gold, light yellow, dark mushroom-beige. Cotton pearl in the same tone as the fabric. (This design could also be worked in shades of any other color.)

Cut the fabric into two circles 18″ across. The second one is for the lining. This allows a 1″ seam allowance all around, which is too much, but do not trim away the excess until you are ready to attach the lining in case you make any error in centering.

1. Draw the complete design on a large sheet of heavy tracing paper.
2. Draw a 7″ circle in the center of the paper. Use a dessert plate as your pattern. Draw another circle ⅜″ outside of this circle. These are your guidelines for the herringbone-stitch frame encircling the center design. Use an 11″ plate to draw the inside line of the outer circle, and then draw another circle ⅜″ outside that one.
3. The central design is given full-size. Add the remaining few lines free-hand to fill out the circle.
4. Select the letters you need from an *alef-bet* in the

PLATE I: Star quilt

PLATE II: Necktie
patchwork *tallit* bag

PLATE III: The Lion and the Dove *tallit* bag

PLATE IV: *Mazzal Tov* doll

PLATE V: *Shtetl* tablecloth

PLATE VI: Matching grape appliqué cloth

PLATE VII: "Joseph's Coat" cushion

PLATE VIII: Jerusalem   cushion

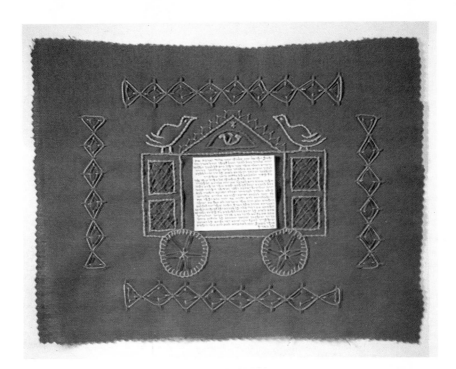

Plate IX: *Mezuzah*

Plate X: Needlepoint *mizrah*

PLATE XI: Crewel *mizrah*

PLATE XII: Two Boys on a
Tricycle appliqué

PLATE XIII: Flag with wheeled ark

PLATE XIV: Simhat Torah flag
with *lamed* and *bet*

PLATE XV: The *hupah*

FIGURE 73: Pattern for the *hallah* cover

Appendix, using my inscription ("Blessed art Thou, O Lord our God, who hast sanctified the Sabbath") or any you like. If you prefer, the flowers can completely encircle the design, with no words. Or the last verses from the Book of Proverbs, in English or Hebrew, which are traditionally recited by the husband to his wife at the beginning of the Sabbath are appropriate:

> A woman of valour who can find?
> For her price is far above rubies. . . .
> Her children rise up, and call her blessed;
> Her husband also, and he praiseth her:
> 'Many daughters have done valiantly,
> But thou excellest them all" (Proverbs 31:10, 28–29).

The design could also be framed (either round or squared off) and given to a mother or mother-in-law as a gift.

5. Using dressmaker's carbon paper, transfer the design to the fabric. Spray lightly with fixative.

Embroidery: Use three strands of embroidery floss for the entire design.

dark brown: both circles in herringbone stitch; stems of flowers, outline of woman, knives, small dishes, and table legs in outline stitch; inside branches of candelabra have three running stitches in each, and five or six in the oil container which feeds it

medium brown: lettering in closed buttonhole stitch; tablecloth in outline stitch; woman's dress in cross stitches and some straight stitches on hem of dress; flowers: the centers are French knots, and tiny straight stitches over the tips of the petals after they have been done

gold: flower petals are lazy daisy stitch; goblets, chandelier, dress, and apron embroidery are in outline stitch. Other apron embroidery is two rows of straight stitches

FIGURE 74: Patterns for flowers

beige: both windows and outline of floor tiles are in outline stitch; floor-tile filler is in a detached feather stitch.

When the embroidery is complete, iron carefully on the
reverse side on a surface padded with terrycloth toweling. Trim
the fabric to a 17″ circle, making certain to keep the design
centered. Clip the edge of both lining and embroidered part
every inch or so. Pin the two pieces together (right sides together) and seam closed, leaving 4″ or 5″ unsewn to enable
you to turn the cloth right side out again. Sew remainder closed

FIGURE 75: Pattern for the miniature *hallah* cover

by hand. Iron edge carefully. Add any type of edging you like, or leave it plain.

The edging I used was a row of closed buttonhole stitches worked in cotton pearl, with a row of single crochet worked into that. Simple scallops were made by crocheting a five-stitch chain and securing it by taking the sixth stitch into the preceding row. More rows could be added if desired.

The miniature cloth is made in the same way as the large one. Transfer the letters to an 8½" circle of fabric. Add additional flowers to complete the wreath. After the design is embroidered, line the embroidery with a matching circle of fabric. The letters say *shabbat*.

DOUBLE HALLAH COVER

This *hallah* cloth is twice the usual size. It was made to accommodate a congregation-size *hallah* or the two loaves used by many people to celebrate Shabbat. Using two loaves of *hallah* reminds us that a double portion of manna was given to the Hebrews in the wilderness on Friday so they would not profane the Sabbath by working to gather food on the day of rest. Some say that covering the *hallah* with a cloth is reminiscent of the dew that covered the manna in the desert. Others maintain that since the blessing for wine precedes that for the bread, covering the *hallah* with a cloth prevents God from becoming "confused." I like both of these interpretations— one for its legendary associations, and the other because it so well reflects the Jew's intimate relationship with, and personal concern for, his God.

The design for this cloth was done by making a paper-cut and then drawing around it. It appears complex because of the repetition of the forms. It is based on an abstracted *hallah*, surrounded by ten bunches of grapes and two *menorot*, all encircled by a crown. The grapes were used because of their association with the sanctification of the Sabbath; the candles,

FIGURE 76: Double *hallah* cover

FIGURE 77: Paper-cut on which the double *hallah* cover was based

EACH SQUARE = 1"

CENTER LINE

CENTER LINE

FIGURE 78: Pattern for the double *hallah* cover, with grid

because the weekly holiday is inaugurated with the lighting of the candles, and the crown as symbolic of the Lord who gave us the Sabbath.

FINISHED SIZE: 22½" x 28½" oval

MATERIALS:
1⅓" yard of 36"-wide fabric or proportionate amount of wider fabric
embroidery floss in a contrasting color
2⅓" yards edging if desired

Cut the fabric into two rectangles, each 24" x 30". One-quarter of the design is given in Figure 78; it is half the size that you will need. Enlarge the design to measure 9" x 12". Then repeat it four times on a large sheet of paper, reversing it twice to make the full oval. Carefully match center lines. When the drawing is complete to your liking, transfer it to the fabric with dressmaker's tracing paper. Spray with fixative.

This design could be worked in many different ways. The possibilities include filling in the entire design with satin stitch, using many colors for a multicolor effect; or embroidering rows of chain stitch to fill in most of the pattern. On the cloth shown here, the linear quality of the drawing was emphasized by using only the outline stitch, which created a lacy effect not unlike wrought-iron grillwork.

When the embroidery is completed, carefully fold it in fourths and cut away the fabric 3" all around the outside of the design. This will give you the oval. Cut a second oval from the remaining fabric to match the embroidered one, and sew the two together, right sides together, leaving an 8" opening. Clip the seam allowance where necessary to insure a smoothly curved edge, and turn the completed cloths right side out. Slip-stitch the remaining seam closed. Add commercial trim if desired, or make your own.

SHTETL *TABLECLOTH: A DESIGN FROM MY GRANDFATHER'S SILVER CUP*

When my father's father came to the United States in January 1905, he left behind in the Ukraine his old mother, three sons, and a pregnant wife. My father was born in June of that same year. Like so many Eastern European Jews, my grandfather left his impoverished village to try for a better life in America.

A little more than a year later, he was back for a visit with his family. He had returned to have a last look at his village and to prepare his wife and children for what they all hoped would be a prompt exodus from the Ukraine to America. *Der Zayde* [the grandfather], as my sister and I later called

FIGURE 79: My grandfather's silver cup

him, then a man in his early thirties, told his eager listeners how he had arrived in New York and found that it was impossible for him to exist there. The big city was oppressive, and in order to earn a living one had to work on the Sabbath. That he simply would not do. So with a like-minded friend, and 32¢ in his pocket, he walked and hitchhiked (if that's what it was called in 1905) to Maine. The town he picked to settle in was Rockland,* then, as now, a fishing village and marketing center for the neighboring farms. With his meager resources he had become an "I-cash-clothes-man." Ironically, there, in a totally Christian environment, he felt he could more easily live a full Jewish life. (Fifty years later, in his eighties, he still insisted that he could not speak English, although he carried on complex business affairs in his New England town.) For him Rockland, Maine, became his new *shtetl*.

Der Zayde returned to Maine after remaining with his family in the Ukraine for a few years. He left my Grandmother Raisel pregnant with yet another son. He promised to send them money for transportation and boat tickets as soon as possible. It was more than ten years, in 1920, before that promise could be fulfilled. A great many things happened in those years in both of the "family villages." Transportation money was sent and disappeared in an apparent fraud. The two oldest sons and my father's mother died, leaving the three youngest boys in the care of my grandfather's mother. It was she who accompanied them on their journey to Maine. Two other families left the village with them, their few belongings wrapped in bundles.

They got as far as Warsaw when the money ran out, and they waited there for more to come from Maine. A year later it did. On the boat coming over, when a *minyan* [quorum of ten men] met for services, it was found that my father—more than fourteen years old—had never been called to the Torah

---

* Imagine his delight years later when his granddaughter married a man of that name (no relation to the town)!

because, with all the disruptions in the family, it had not been possible earlier. So, in the steerage section of a boat in the mid-Atlantic, my father was called to the Torah for the first time, and became a *bar mitzvah*. As is customary at all the great occasions of life, somehow a festive meal was prepared.

One of the families with whom they had left their village was also on the boat, but the other had not received money in time and so remained behind to wait. When their funds finally did arrive, the United States had passed the Immigration Act of 1924, limiting the number of people allowed to enter from Eastern Europe. This family emigrated to Argentina. My father never mentioned them to me, but when my husband was in the U.S. Foreign Service and we were assigned to Argentina, he gave me a slip of paper with a name and address and asked me to give my regards if I had time. That curious meeting in the lobby of a Buenos Aires hotel quickened my interest in Eastern European Jewish life. I spoke in Yiddish with this boy-hood friend of my father, now quite gray, his expressions colored by Spanish, mine by English, tears streaming down our faces the whole time. His first question, *"Vos macht Yiddle-fun-der-bergle?"* ["How is little Joe from the hill doing?"], was answered somehow by my being there as the wife of an American diplomat with my two little boys who he insisted looked just like my father had as a child. A few days later we shared the Sabbath meal at his home with his family and received careful instructions to tell my father that he also had found a good life in a new land.

When my father, his two brothers, and the old grandmother arrived in Rockland, Maine, after the sea voyage and a two-day train ride, they found that my grandfather had really settled into American life. After receiving word that his wife had died, he had waited a respectful period of time and then married a woman from Boston, where there was a large Jewish community. They had two young American children. The old-clothes business had expanded into a junk and scrap-metal business which would become very profitable during World

FIGURE 80: The complete border for the *shtetl* tablecloth

War II. More Jewish families had come to town, so an abandoned church was bought and turned into a lovely little white frame synagogue and part-time religious school.

In the bundle they had carried with them from the *shtetl* was all that remained of that former life: a peasant-style bedspread made by my grandmother and a set of three little silver cups. The bedspread is crocheted in black cotton, with multicolor wool woven through it, forming flowers and the following inscription in Ukrainian: "Woman's Hand Work 1909 R. SH." (the last, my grandmother's initials). The silver cups are of a common type which were commercially available in Eastern Europe at the end of the last century and the beginning of this one. Because they were inexpensive they were bought by the Jewish families in the Pale of Settlement, and when the Jews emigrated they were often the only possession of any value, and so were packed into bundles and brought to America. These cups, which were not originally "Jewish," have almost become Jewish by conversion through many Jewish celebrations and making the long trip to new Diasporas. Reproductions of them are sold in Jewish gift shops.

When my grandfather died in 1956, the bedspread was given to me because I had been married the year before, and the three silver cups were divided among his sons. When my first son was born in 1958 and named for my grandfather, my father gave his silver cup to the new David.

The cup is engraved with a few skillful lines depicting hilly countryside, village houses, and a little foliage. Interlaced arcs formed by tiny dots and dashes provide "windows" through which to gaze at the simply depicted view. The silver and antique value are minimal, but the scene depicted is priceless. For the humble *shtetl* was the kingdom of the Jew in exile.

I have taken this scene and enlarged it to use as the border design for the embroidered tablecloth that follows. The engraved lines on the silver cup lend themselves very well to reinterpretation in simple running and outline stitches, which are used throughout. The design is a repetition of two basic

FIGURE 81. The *shtetl* tablecloth on the table

motifs: one of the village and the other of foliage. Either one could be used separately if desired, or any number of them combined to make objects of different sizes.

The finished size of this cloth is 62″ square because my dining-room table is 42″ square. This cloth is most effective if it is made so that the embroidered seams holding the borders to the center of the cloth lie just at the outer edge of the table. If you prefer, however, the design can be drawn on a purchased tablecloth that already fits your table; then you will eliminate the construction aspect of this cloth and only do the embroidery.

For the cloth as shown, you will need 3¼ yards of 44″- or 45″-wide fabric. Cut the fabric as shown in the diagram, and add an additional 1½″ all around for seam allowances. I used purple embroidery on a chartreuse green cloth.

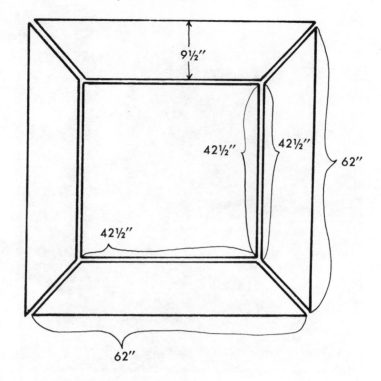

FIGURE 82: Measurements for the *shtetl* tablecloth

Each border is made up of 10 motif repetitions plus additional running stitches at either end to fill out the corner.

Using a sheet of paper half as long as your border (in my case it was 31″ long), draw as many motifs as you need for half the border. Kitchen shelving paper is very useful for this, or tape together typing paper. The paper should be strong and slightly transparent, since you will use it to go over the design from both sides when tracing it onto the cloth. Be careful to match the arcs where they join between motifs so the bottom and top line will come out straight.

Pin the drawing to one of the border panels, or to the tablecloth you already own. Leave the same amount of space at the top and bottom. Line up the edge of the drawing with the center line of the fabric. Slide dressmaker's tracing paper face down between the drawing and the fabric and with a

FIGURE 83: Patterns for the designs from the silver cup

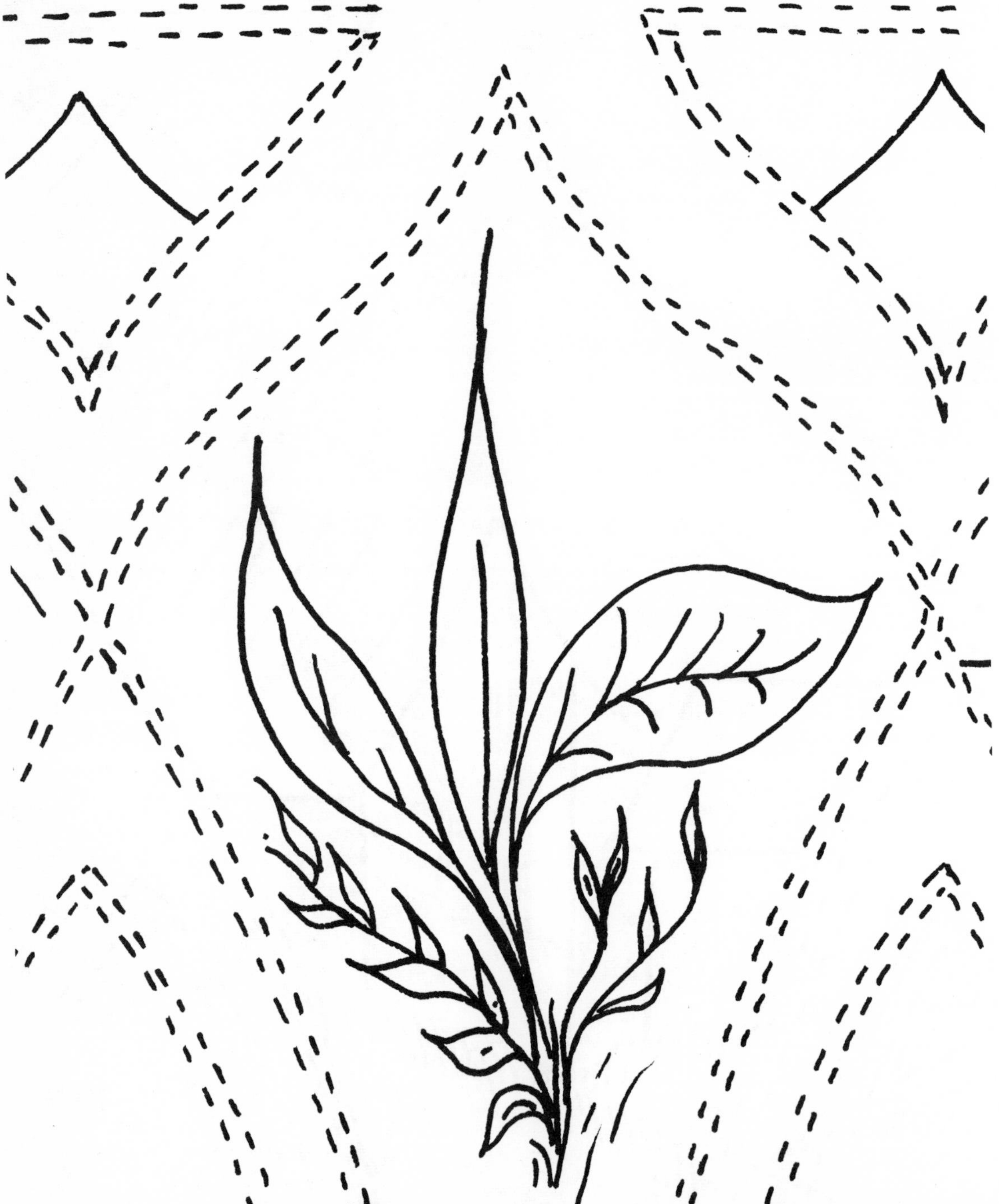

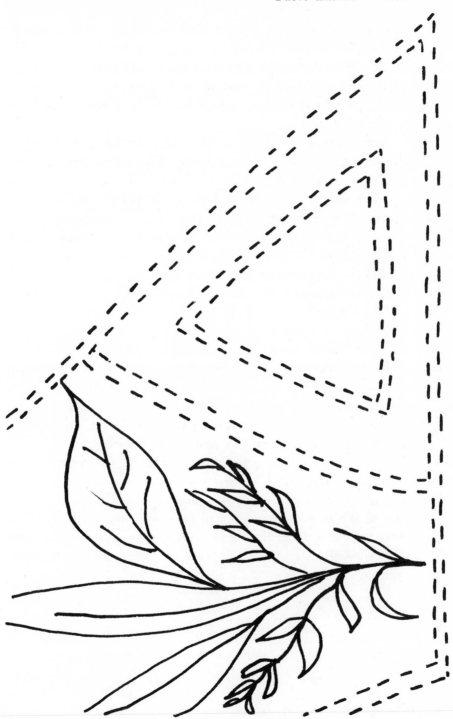

ballpoint pen trace the design onto the fabric. After completing one half, unpin the drawing and turn it over. Pin it onto the other half of the fabric. The drawing should show through the paper, and you will be able to draw a mirror image on the other half of the border. Repeat for the remaining three sides of the tablecloth.

I used cotton pearl thread, but three strands of embroidery thread could be used if you desire. The embroidery is done entirely in running and outline stitches, with the exception of a few lazy daisy stitches for the smaller leaves and an occasional French knot. Do not be concerned with keeping everything uniform, both as you draw and as you sew. If every view is a little different, it adds liveliness to the general effect.

When the embroidery is completed, iron it face down on a padded surface. Turn under and iron all the seam allowances on the border pieces and on the center panel. Working on a large table, pin the edge of the center panel to a long strip of paper (again, shelf paper is handy)—this will hold the two pieces together while you work. Pin one of the border pieces in place, leaving ⅛″ space between the two edges. Make certain that the centers and corners are matched. Starting at one end of the center panel, attach the border strip, using alternating buttonhole stitches to join the two pieces.

Since the seam will get the most wear, use twice the amount of thread for it that you used for the embroidery: that is, six strands of embroidery floss or a double thread of cotton pearl. Do the diagonal corners after all four sides have been attached. The hem was done by folding under the edge of the seam allowance and securing it in place with two rows of running stitches.

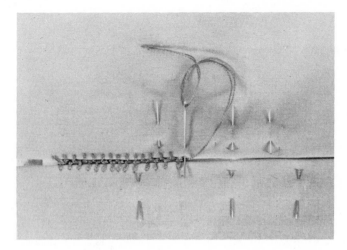

FIGURE 84: The buttonhole insertion stitch in progress

FIGURE 85: Detail of a corner of the tablecloth

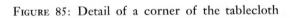

GRAPE APPLIQUÉ

And wine that maketh glad the heart.
Psalm 104:15

When the Jews were wandering in the wilderness after leaving Egypt, twelve spies were sent into the Promised Land to see what would be in store for them. Two returned laden with gigantic clusters of grapes carried on a stave between them. This was truly the Promised Land. The symbol of two men carrying a huge bunch of grapes is now used by the Israeli Tourist Office and also by the Carmel wineries.

The Promised Land is described in Deuteronomy 8:8 as "a land of wheat and barley, and vines and fig-trees and pomegranates; a land of olive-trees and honey." With the fig tree, palm, and pomegranate (and to a lesser extent the olive branch, barley, and wheat), the grape vine became one of the characteristic Jewish design motifs.

Golden grape vines ornamented the Temple walls and doors. Grapes and vines were used as emblems on coins minted during the First Revolt against Imperial Rome in 66 C.E. and were used decoratively in murals and mosaics in early Palestinian synagogues; they have been found in the Jewish catacombs in Rome.

Even though wine is mentioned in the Bible in connection with Noah's drunkenness (Genesis 9:20–24) and as being instrumental to the incestuous activity of Lot and his two daughters (Genesis 18:30–35), the Jewish attitude toward the drinking of wine has always been that it is one of life's legitimate pleasures, since it "cheereth God and man" (Judges 9:13). While excessive drinking is traditionally encouraged on Purim (until one can no longer distinguish between Haman and Mordecai) and Simhat Torah, moderation at other times is taught from early childhood. The universally acknowledged

FIGURE 86: Grape appliqué cloth

low rate of Jewish alcoholism testifies to the wisdom of this approach. Drinking wine after a blessing is the most often-repeated ritual observance. Wine is a symbol of joy at festive occasions and holidays, and it also has a place at the meal of consolation offered to mourners.

This oval cloth was made as a companion to the *shtetl* tablecloth. It is made of the same chartreuse cotton fabric, and the grapes are cut from purple fabric which is similar to the shade of purple used in the embroidery of the cloth. It can be used as a *hallah* cover, centerpiece, tray cover, or even made into a cushion.

The design itself could be used for a variety of objects. The cloth can be enlarged for a tablecloth with the design as the center. Clusters of grapes and vines could be arranged as a border design or corner embellishments for a tablecloth, bedspread, or curtains. The grapes could be any shade of blue, purple, red, or even green or yellow. For a totally different effect, the background fabric or that of the vines could be patterned.

The finished cloth is 21″ x 26″. You will need two slightly larger rectangles as your background fabric. The second one is for the lining and could be of a different fabric. If you are using this as a cushion design, you could repeat the design on the back as well. The edging is a bias strip cut from the same fabric used to make the grapes.

Use a twenty-five-cent piece as the pattern for the thirty-eight grapes. Draw around the quarter with a white dressmaker's pencil and cut the circles out, leaving a ¼″ seam allowance outside the drawn line. In sewing them on, do not try overly hard to keep them perfectly round or they will look very artificial.

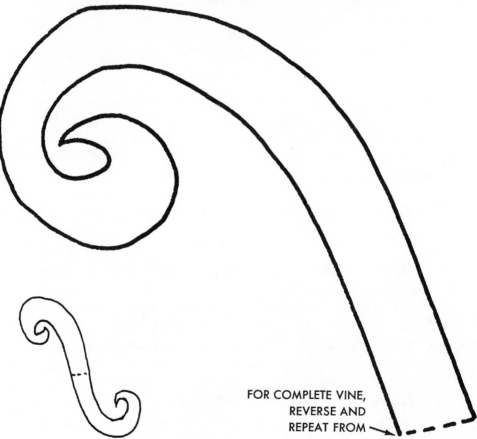

FOR COMPLETE VINE,
REVERSE AND
REPEAT FROM

FIGURE 87: Pattern for the scroll vine

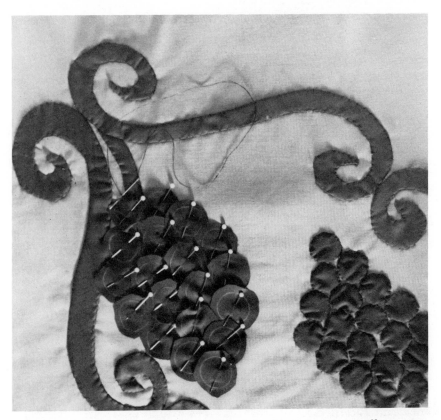

FIGURE 88: When the grapes are pinned in place, their seam allowances overlap

Half of the vine is given here. After you have drawn it, reverse its position to create an elongated S-shaped scroll. Using this scroll as a pattern, cut four vines from dark fabric (I used a forest green), making certain to leave a seam allowance of about ¼″ all around to be turned under as you sew the pieces in place. Cut small bias strips to use for the stems.

Arrange the pieces diagonally across the rectangle and pin them in place. It is better to pin than to baste when you appliqué: the pieces become smaller as you turn the edges under and sew them down. If they are pinned rather than basted, you can easily move other pieces around and make any adjustments that seem necessary.

Contrasting thread could be used if desired, but I used mercerized cotton in an inconspicuous, matching shade to blind-stitch the pieces to the background fabric. When all the pieces are sewn in place, fold the rectangle in fourths and carefully trim the corner fabric into a curve; when unfolded, this will give you the oval shape.

Cut the lining fabric to match, and bind the whole thing with a bias strip of fabric.

INFORMAL HOLIDAY TABLECLOTH

There are a number of holidays in the Jewish calendar that lend themselves to informal celebration; they are by their very nature relaxed and gay. This rustic tablecloth was made with Sukkot, Lag Ba-Omer, Purim, and Hanukkah in mind. Purim and Hanukkah are both historical holidays commemorating Jewish survival in the face of persecution: physical survival in the case of Purim, and spiritual survival in the case of Hanukkah.

Though the exact origins of Lag Ba-Omer (which takes place in the spring, thirty-three days after Pesah) are obscure, it is often called The Scholar's Holiday, because it is said that the young students of Rabbi Akiba (ca. 40–ca. 135), during the Roman occupation of Israel, would go to the woods with bows and arrows and other sporting equipment, pretending to picnic but really to study Torah, which was forbidden by the Romans, and to discuss politics, as this was the time of the Bar Kokhba uprising. In the Jewish villages of Eastern Europe, the children used to picnic and play "Jews and Romans" on Lag Ba-Omer much as American children play "cowboys and Indians." Today Lag Ba-Omer is still the occasion for picnics, and this cloth would be fun for outdoor use.

Another outdoor holiday is Sukkot, an autumn harvest festival, which, like most of the Jewish holidays that grew out

FIGURE 89: Holiday tablecloth on picnic table

FIGURE 90: Appliquéd central square of the patchwork holiday table-cloth

of ancient pastoral or agricultural festivals, took on a deeper meaning by commemorating a historic event. The Festival of Tabernacles reminds us of life in temporary shelters during the forty years of wandering in the desert after the Exodus from Egypt. The American holiday of Thanksgiving was modeled after Sukkot by the Pilgrims who, in gratitude for their harvest, identified with the Children of Israel and felt that, in America, they had found the Promised Land.

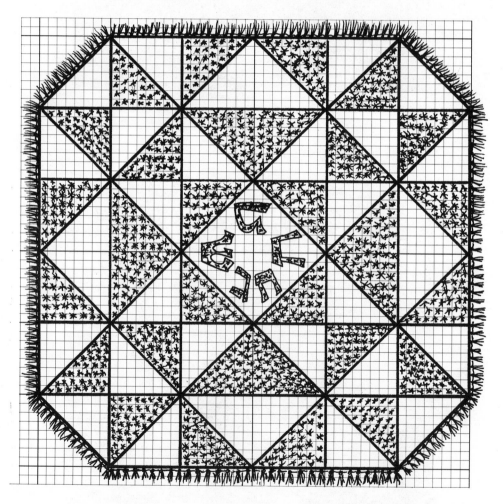

FIGURE 91: Pattern for the holiday tablecloth, with grid

FINISHED SIZE: 54" square (with or without corners), plus fringe

MATERIALS:

2 yards of solid-color fabric

2 yards of print fabric

8 yards of washable cotton fringe. If you decide to make the tablecloth with square rather than clipped corners, an additional yard of fringe is suggested. I've allowed more fringe than the actual measurements indicate, because it should be applied with some easing to allow for shrinkage. Also, it tends to stretch when being measured.

Following the usual patchwork procedure, make cardboard patterns of the pieces you need. Draw around them with a sharp pencil on the reverse side of the fabric. Cut pieces out, leaving a ⅜" or ½" seam allowance outside the pencil line.

1. Make two cardboard squares: a 9" square and a 12¾" square.

2. Cut the 9" square diagonally in half, thereby producing two triangles which measure 9" x 9" x 12¾". Cut 24 of these triangles from the printed fabric.

3. Use the 12¾" pattern to cut one large square from the solid fabric. Then cut this same cardboard pattern in half diagonally, making two large triangles. Use one of these as your pattern to cut 4 large triangles of solid fabric and 4 of the print.

4. Use the letters חג שמח ("joyous holiday") in the diagrams as your guide for making the cardboard patterns. Draw around the cardboard shapes on the *right* side of the print fabric. Your pencil line will be the fold line when you appliqué the letters in place. Leave enough room between the letters to allow a ¼" seam allowance.

5. Place the letters on the large solid square as shown in Figures 90 and 91. Pin in place with a pin in the center and "leg" of each letter. Then turn under along fold line and pin edges. Clip seam allowance at corners and

FIGURE 92: Patterns for the letters for the holiday tablecloth

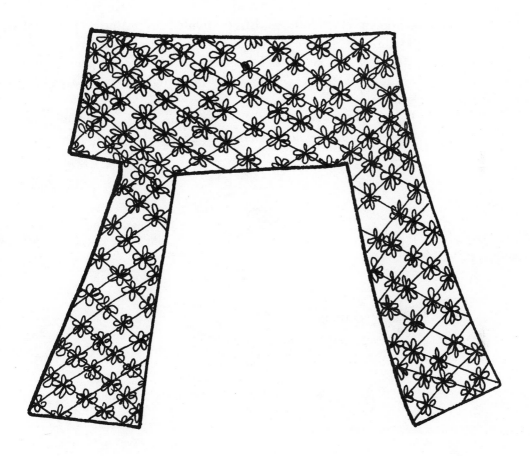

curves, placing the pins across in an up-and-down position, perpendicular to the fold line. (This causes the
shapes to stretch less.) Stitch in place, using an ordinary
hemming stitch or running stitch, or a more elaborate
embroidery stitch such as herringbone or buttonhole.

6. The assembly of the triangles will be simpler if you
   think of the cloth as being divided into thirds and
   assemble it in three panels, keeping the diagram in front
   of you as you work. It is important to follow the pencil
   line on the back as your seam line in order to insure
   perfect points.

7. Fringe can be put on with or without a zigzag attach-
   ment on your sewing machine or by hand.

Pesah—Passover

EVERY YEAR, for more than 3000 years, Jewish families around the world have reenacted the Exodus from Egyptian slavery in a home service which is the oldest continually celebrated religious ceremony in the world. Some scholars believe that the offering of the Pesah sacrifice was actually practiced by the Hebrew tribes when they were nomadic shepherds *before* their enslavement in Egypt, and that it was in order for them to be able to perform their ancient spring rite of sacrificing a lamb and smearing the tent posts with its blood that Moses petitioned the Pharaoh for freedom. The agricultural festival of unleavened bread was then incorporated into the Pesah celebration after the Jews settled in the Promised Land.

Like all symbols and practices that come down to us from antiquity, the Passover customs are older than their interpretations. In its constant reinterpretation of traditions in the light of modern experience, Passover pours old wine into new bottles, creating a home ceremony unsurpassed for its profundity, its simple beauty, and its ability to stir the emotions. As the Passover story is retold and the symbolic food explained, we feel not only as though our ancestors were redeemed from slavery but as though we, too, have personally come out of bondage. We feel ourselves to be a link in the unbroken chain of history that began even before the Exodus from Egypt in the thirteenth century B.C.E., for not only once but, according to the Haggadah, in "every generation they rise against us to

157

destroy us; but the Holy One (blessed be He) delivers us from their hand."

The ceremony we follow today is almost unchanged since the Middle Ages, although individual families and groups make changes and include readings that have special meaning for themselves. In recent years it has become customary to add a word of remembrance for the Jews slaughtered by the Nazis and especially for those of the Warsaw Ghetto who staged an uprising against overwhelming odds on the eve of Pesah in 1943. Another recent practice is that of setting aside a *"Matzah of Hope"* as a sign of solidarity with the three million Jews of the Soviet Union who are denied religious liberty. These Russian Jews have added another verse to the traditional Pesah song *"Dayaynu"*: "He who has brought us forth from the slavery of Egypt will deliver us from the slavery of Russia.*

The Passover ceremonial meal is called a Seder ("order," for a definite procedure is followed) among Ashkenazic Jews, and Haggadah ("telling" or "narration") among Sephardic Jews. The special book containing the prayers, stories, and ceremonial procedures to be followed is also called the Haggadah. The table service is in a certain sense a theatrical event. The children are at one and the same time the audience and the featured players. The Seder is designed to fulfill the injunction to "tell thy son in that day, saying: It is because of that which the Lord did for me when I came forth out of Egypt" (Exodus 13:8).

The midrashic parable of the four sons related during the course of the evening recognizes that there are many different kinds of children. The father is enjoined to explain the meanings of the festival differently to each child, depending upon its capacity to absorb and learn. The intelligent child (that delight of Jewish families) should be fully instructed in all the details and nuances of history and observances. The child of limited capacity is taught by pointing at the ceremonial foods

* "Silent No More," recorded by Theodore Bikel, Star Record Company in cooperation with the American Jewish Congress.

and explaining that "all of this is because of what the Lord did for me when I came out of Egypt." The story of the Exodus from slavery is told simply to the young child who does not know how to ask. The dialogue between the father and the son who is hostile to the proceedings of the evening is summed up in two verses from the "Ballad of the Four Sons" sung to the melody of "Clementine" which I first heard at a community Seder on a United States Air Force base in Torrejon, Spain:

> Then did sneer the son so wicked,
> "What does all this mean to *you?*"
> And the father's voice was bitter
> As his grief and anger grew.

> "If yourself you don't consider
> As a Son of Israel,
> Then for you this has no meaning,
> You could be a slave as well."

The leader of the Seder has a cushion at his seat so he can "recline" during the festive meal. In some homes a pillow is provided for every male over thirteen and in other families there is a pillow for everyone. This practice goes back to hellenistic times when it was customary at luxurious feasts for free men to lie on sofas. Since this style of life depended upon a slave economy, the rabbis during the Middle Ages sought to abolish this custom at Pesah, seeing in it a sign of weakness and decadence. They were not successful, however, and it remains with us today as a symbol of our freedom.

"JOSEPH'S COAT" CUSHION

The cushion shown here was made in the American colonial patchwork pattern known as "Joseph's Coat." I chose this pattern because it was due to Joseph that the Hebrew tribes went to Egypt in the first place.

FIGURE 93: "Joseph's Coat" patchwork cushion

The pillow cover was made in solid shades of red, blue, off-white, and purple. Another way to make this is to use an assortment of scrap fabric or to cut some of the units from patterned fabric and others from solid colors. The important thing about this design is that the 32 small triangles are of one tone, either darker or lighter than the other shapes, because they effectively provide the structure of the design by serving as a background. (This could be another place to use up retired neckties.)

FINISHED SIZE: 18″ square cover for a 16″ pillow

MATERIALS:

one 16″ pillow

(Yardage estimates are generous to allow for possible error in cutting or drawing. Four colors of 36″-wide fabric are used.)

1/6 yard red

⅓ yard blue

1/6 yard off-white

½ yard + 1″ (19″ cut from a 36″-wide yard) purple

Cut a 19″ square of purple for the back of the pillow case. This allows ½″ seam allowance.

Cut four blue strips, each 2½″ x 19″. This is for the border and allows for mitering the corners.

Make cardboard or sandpaper patterns in the sizes given below, and cut the necessary squares and triangles from the four different fabrics as indicated.

UNIT C-8   UNIT A-1   UNIT B-4   UNIT E-32
UNIT D-4   UNIT C-8   UNIT E-4

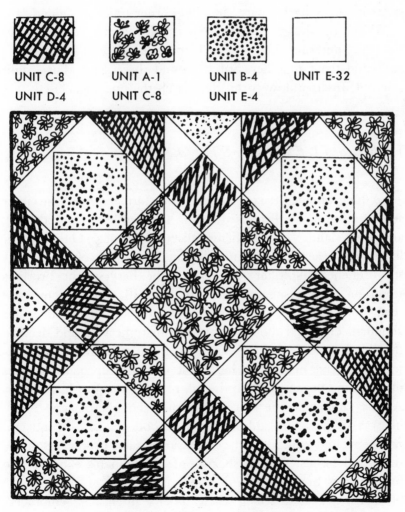

FIGURE 94: The arrangement of the patchwork cushion

UNIT A (4¼″ square): 1 red
UNIT B (3″ square): 4 blue
UNIT C (triangle, half of a 3″ square): 8 red, 8 purple
UNIT D (2⅛″ square): 4 purple
UNIT E (triangle, half of a 2⅛″ square): 4 blue, 32 off-white

Although everyone eventually discovers her own best way of working, I find it simplest to assemble the four corner units first, then the four center bands. These bands are joined to the sides of the central square, and the corner units are added last.

When the design is assembled, attach the blue strips around the sides, mitering the corners. Place right sides of the pillow's back and front together. Stitch around three sides. Turn right side out. Insert pillow form. Slip-stitch the opening closed.

JERUSALEM CUSHION

A long time ago two brothers, both farmers, lived on either side of a hill in the Promised Land. The brothers worked hard, and their land yielded them substantial crops. One brother lived alone; the other was married and had many children. One star-drenched night, at the end of the harvest, the brothers stood on their respective sides of the hill and contemplated their good fortune. The unmarried brother looked over his abundant crop and thought how fortunate he was, and decided that his brother, who had so many more mouths to feed, deserved to have more than he. So he gathered up many sheaves of grain and began to climb the hill to bring them to his brother. At the same time the married brother thought of how lucky he was to have, in addition to his good crops, a wonderful family around him. He felt compassion for his brother's solitary state, and he also loaded sheaves of grain on his shoulders to bring to his brother. At midnight, at the top of the hill, the brothers met and, seeing each other's intentions, embraced. When God saw the concern and love of the brothers for one

FIGURE 95: Jerusalem cushion

another, He chose that hill to be the location of Jerusalem—the City of Peace.

This lovely legend, which I heard years ago, illustrates how the Jewish nation in its wanderings has always romanticized Jerusalem and longed to return there. The earthly Jerusalem is thought of as a reflection of a heavenly Jerusalem. It is often said that when God gave beauty to the world, He gave nine-tenths of it to Jerusalem.

Because the closing words of the Seder, "Next year in Jerusalem," are so pregnant with meaning and emotion, I chose them as the basis for the design of this Passover cushion. The crenellated shapes of the letters are meant to suggest the walled Old City, and the laid-and-couched stitch to resemble masonry.

MATERIALS:

12" x 16" pillow
2 rectangles of fabric 15" x 19" (this allows for fullness of the pillow and provides a ½" seam allowance all around)
2 yards of upholstery corded piping
15 (yes, 15) skeins of embroidery floss: off-white
1 spool No. 8 cotton pearl thread: off-white
1 spool No. 5 cotton pearl thread: contrasting color (I used red)

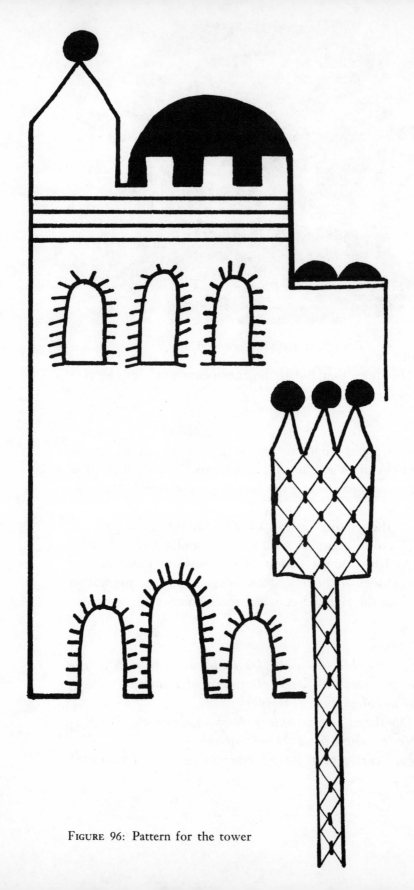

FIGURE 96: Pattern for the tower

EACH SQUARE = 1"

FIGURE 97: Pattern for the Jerusalem cushion, with grid

1. Using the crenellated letters found in the Appendix as a guide, draw the letters you need on a 12″ x 16″ sheet of heavy tracing paper. Draw the tower in the remaining space, or invent your own architectural details. Notice that some of the letters have been changed slightly: this was done to simplify the composition. With so many letters close together, the overall effect—that of the walled city—is more important than that each letter have the same number of crenellations or that certain curves be preserved. For variety, three of the letters are topped with points rather than crenellations for a crown effect. The *lamed* and *he* on the top line have been expanded by almost one-half their width. As noted in the *alef-bet* Appendix, this device to achieve balance in design can be used with the letters *resh*, *dalet*, *he*, *bet*, *tav*, and *lamed*.

2. When the drawing is complete, use dressmaker's tracing paper and trace the drawing onto the fabric, being careful to center it. Spray with fixative.

3. All the letters are done with the laid-and-couched stitch. Use all six strands of embroidery floss as it comes from the skein for the laid stitches. Use the matching cotton pearl thread for the long holding stitches, and the contrasting cotton pearl for the small couching stitches that hold everything in place (Fig. 19). Go around each letter with an outline stitch.

    The dome and ornamental spheres are all worked in satin stitch. The tower is all outline stitch, with the exception of the doors and windows which are a buttonhole stitch.

4. Iron lightly, face down on a surface padded with toweling.

5. Sew the upholstery cording to the embroidered side along the seam allowance.

6. Place lining over embroidery, right sides together. Seam, including the cording's seam allowance, along three sides. Turn right side out. Insert pillow form and sew the remaining seam together by hand.

This design could also be worked in needlepoint. For appliqué, the letters should be simplified further.

HAND TOWEL

The Seder begins with the *kiddush*, a blessing chanted over the first cup of wine (there will be four cups of wine in the course of the evening), which proclaims the holiness of the festival. After the *kiddush* the leader of the Seder washes his hands. A pitcher, bowl, and towel are brought to him. A little later in the service everyone at the table washes his or her hands. The washing of the hands is a symbolic act of purification by the participants in the Seder. In the days of the Temple, the priests would wash their hands before approaching the altar; now each Jew symbolically acts as a priest.

The hand towel shown here was inspired by Psalm 134:2, "Lift up your hands to the sanctuary, And bless ye the Lord." This verse is usually recited before the blessing for washing the hands. The verse, or parts of it, could be embroidered on the towel in English or Hebrew. Either the words indicating

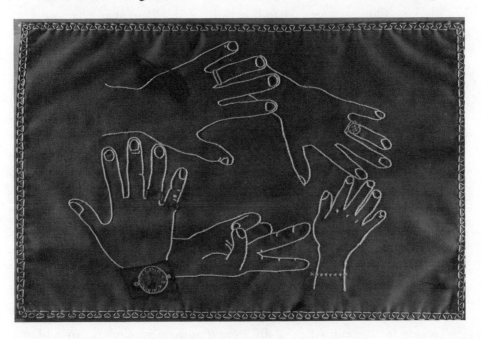

FIGURE 98: Hand towel

the handwashing ritual or the actual blessing could be used as well. I chose not to have any inscription on my towel because its function speaks for itself (also, it is made as part of a Passover set, and several of the other pieces have inscriptions).

No drawing is provided for this project. Use the hands of your own family and/or friends. Trace each person's hand on a separate sheet of paper. Decide before beginning how many right and left hands you will want for your design. Roughly cut the drawings outside the drawn line and rearrange them on a large sheet of paper until you find a pleasing arrangement. They can be made to form a circle, be upraised in praise or prayer, lined up open-palmed, or overlapped. The possibilities are limited only by your own imagination. Hands are incredibly expressive: almost the whole range of human emotion can be expressed in gestures. Once you have the cut-out hands arranged on the master sheet, use carbon paper to get them all drawn onto it. Add any details for realism or to balance the design. Our teenager's hand is only a shade smaller than my husband's, and in order to differentiate between them more than the rings alone would have indicated, I added my son's wristwatch (which he really wears on his left wrist).

The hands, rings, and watchband were all worked in chain stitch. Straight stitches were used for the watch numerals. The watch hands are done in outline stitch. The little girl's bracelet was made with double cross stitches, forming an eight-limbed star. The border, which looks very elaborate, is really quite simple. The edge was turned under twice (as an ordinary hem would be) and secured in place with two rows of running stitches ¼″ apart; another color is then threaded through (Fig. 33). Take care to have the second row of stitches alternate with the first so it can be threaded evenly to create the border design.

My towel was done on a piece of fabric 18″ x 26″, which finished to a 16″ x 24″ towel. You might want it longer or wider to accommodate a different family grouping or to add the prayer (or part of it) for handwashing.

AFIKOMEN *BAG*

After the *kiddush* and the handwashing, the spring greens are blessed; and then a feature of the Seder that seems especially designed to interest the children occurs. Three pieces of *matzah* [unleavened bread] enjoy special status. They represent the ancient classes of Israel: Kohanim, Levites, and Israel. These three pieces are placed on the table under a special cover with pockets to hold them, and the other *matzot* are placed under the same cloth or on a different plate. The middle *matzah*

FIGURE 99: Four Sons *afikomen* bag

is broken in two. The largest part is reserved for the *afikomen* (from the Greek word for "dessert") which is a substitute for the last morsel of the sacrificial lamb eaten at the end of the meal. The *afikomen* is hidden by the leader of the ceremony, to be found later by the children. The children keep watching and listening in the hope of finding clues to its whereabouts.

In our family, my husband and I have worked out an elaborate scheme: when I bring him the pitcher and bowl to wash his hands the second time, he discreetly passes me the wrapped *afikomen* and then I hide it in a prearranged place. (Now that I've said this, we'll have to change our plan.) At the end of the meal, while the adults are leisurely sipping their coffee and tea, the children tear the house apart looking for the *afikomen*. The one who finds it is rewarded with a little present. Those who don't find it get the same present as consolation prizes, but the winner gets a badge that says *"Hakham"* [wise one]. When we have the Seder at my father's house, the child who finds the *afikomen* demands a ransom for it from the adults, who try to outbid one another to redeem the "dessert."

Last year, the *afikomen*, wrapped in a napkin, was placed under the rug in the study. It was almost trampled into crumbs by the children in their eagerness, so I decided to make a special bag to contain it, in the hope of receiving it back in better condition in future years.

The design for the bag is based on the parable of the four sons (see pp. 158–59).

FINISHED DIMENSIONS: 10½″ x 5½″

MATERIALS:
red rectangle 6½″ x 12½″
blue rectangle 6½″ x 12½″
off-white embroidery thread
purple cotton pearl thread
cord or ribbon

FIGURE 100: Patterns for the Four Sons

1. Using dressmaker's tracing paper, draw figures of children onto the rectangles of fabric.* Write *afikomen* in Hebrew on one side and in English on the other. Draw two dotted lines across the top of the rectangle: the first line 1¾″ from the top, and the second 2″ from the top. It is important to stagger these dashes for running stitches and to space them evenly in order to be able to thread them decoratively later (see Fig. 33).

2. Lightly spray drawing with fixative.

3. The figures and letters were embroidered in chain stitch. Straight stitches and French knots were used to add variety to the features and hair.

4. Fold the top 1¼″ of the rectangle under to the reverse side. Iron.

5. Stitch this down with purple running stitches along the two dotted lines. Weave white thread in and out of the two rows of stitches as shown in the photographs.

* It would be even better to get your children to draw their own interpretations of the four different types of sons. Figures aren't necessary; faces would be just as amusing.

FIGURE 101: The *afikomen* bag with the embroidery completed and one seam sewn. One side is red, the other blue. The children and letters are embroidered in white

6. With right sides together, stitch the remaining three sides together.
7. Turn right side out and run a cord through the fold at the top of the bag.

CONTEMPORARY MATZAH COVER AND MINIATURE

When the *afikomen* has been broken from the middle *matzah,* the narrative part of the Seder begins with the youngest child present asking the traditional four questions. Whether the questions are asked in Hebrew or the language of the country in which the Seder is taking place, the sight of a shy young child in holiday clothes singing (if possible) the questions asked by so many generations in so many corners of the world seldom leaves a dry eye.

FIGURE 102: *Halayla hazzeh matzah* cover and miniature

The questions begin with a statement of awe:

מה־נשתנה הלילה הזה מכל־הלילות

"How different is this night from all other nights!" I have taken the central phrase "*halaylah hazzeh*" ["this night"] to use as the embroidered inscription on this *matzah* cover.

A *matzah* cover, in reality, is more a container than a cover. It has three pockets made by layering four pieces of cloth. The colors I used—blue, red, purple, and linen—are described in Exodus as those of the original desert Tabernacle. The four layers of the large cloth are secured only at the corners in order to make the *matzah* accessible from any side of the table.

For an 18″ square cloth you will need a 23″ square of fabric for the bottom layer, a 20″ square for the second layer, a 17″ square for the third layer, and a 12½″ square for the top piece which is embroidered before being joined to the other layers.

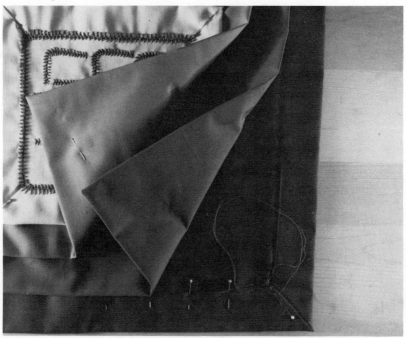

FIGURE 103: The wide hem is blind-stitched in place. The hem of the layer beneath forms the border of the next layer

A 2½" hem is turned up on all four sides of the three bottom squares, and a 1½" hem on the top square. Miter the corners and blind-stitch in place. The hemmed squares will be 18", 15", 12", and 9½" when finished. The *alef-bet* I used was the simplest stick form and was embroidered in Cretan stitch. The same stitch was also used to emphasize the bordering hem of the top layer.

My five-year-old daughter wanted her own *matzah* cover. Using scraps from mine, she made one that will accommodate the tiny 4" round tea *matzot* her dolls enjoy. Rather than hemming the edges, which was too difficult for her, she fringed them. This would be attractive for an adult cloth too, though with some fabrics the fringes tend to become shabby with laundering. The layers were stitched together simply with running stitches, which were also used to embroider the word פסח ["Pesah"] which I wrote for her. The squares for the minature cloth are 11", 9½", 8", and 6½", including the fringes.

TRADITIONAL MATZAH COVER

This traditionally styled *matzah* cover was embroidered with green silk buttonhole twist thread on fine white cotton fabric. The pockets were made by stacking four additional squares of cloth face down on the embroidered square and seaming them together around the two sides and the top. When the embroidery was turned right side out, the layer closest to the top was slip-stitched to it along the open edge, forming a lining for the heavily embroidered piece. The embroidered square measures 14½" when finished. In order not to make the cloth too heavy, I would recommend using cotton batiste lining for the pockets and lining rather than the heavyweight cotton or linen you will use for the top. Handmade Spanish lace 2½" wide was attached all around the top layer with a herringbone stitch.

FIGURE 104: Green-and-white traditional *matzah* cover

The *alef-bet* I used is a slight variation of the traditional one in the Appendix. The center word says "Pesah" and the surrounding inscription is the blessing for *matzot* which can be found in any Haggadah. The wave motif encircling the central word was used as a reminder of the infant Moses being fished out of the water and the opening of the Red Sea to allow the escaping Hebrews to pass through.

Since Pesah takes place in the spring, I chose to have all the foliage in the form of buds rather than fully developed flowers. Spring was also the reason I used green for the embroidery thread.

If you decide to use an inscription encircling the central word, draw an 11″ circle (use a plate to trace around) for the

FIGURE 105: Pattern for the foliage

top line of the letters and a 10″ circle for the base line. Divide the circle into as many sections as there are letters and spaces in the inscription you choose.

The border appears symmetrical but actually is not. I doodled a number of scrolls and flowers as I went along. If you want it to be more regular, repeat the foliage given here, reversing it when a mirror image is required. Because of the lettering, it is especially important to work out the design on paper first and then transfer it to the cloth with dressmaker's tracing paper.

When the four questions have been answered, and the answers elaborated upon with stories, songs, and prayers, the holiday meal is eaten. After the meal, the *afikomen* is searched for, found, and distributed among all participants in the Seder. No more food is served as the Seder continues with prayers of thanksgiving, the drinking of the two final cups of wine, the ceremony of opening the door for the prophet Elijah, and songs of praise.

The final prayer, which concludes the formal part of the Seder, but which is usually followed by the singing of folk songs, provided the phrase for the Passover cushion (p. 162).

לשנה הבאה בירושלים

"The Passover Seder is now complete. . . . As we were privileged to celebrate it tonight, So may we always be worthy to do so. Next year [may we celebrate] in Jerusalem."

The Synagogue

WHILE THE IMPORTANCE and beauty of home celebrations cannot be overemphasized, it is the synagogue that provides the environment for community educational, social, and sacred experiences. Even those Jews who do not consider themselves religious are usually committed to the idea of Jewish group survival; and the synagogue provides the physical place where individuals, who in their daily lives may have very little contact with one another, can come together to share and enrich their common heritage.

In the first twelve years of our marriage, my husband and I moved around a great deal. Military service, graduate school, and then the diplomatic service took us in rapid succession from New York to Japan, Minnesota, Washington, Argentina, and Spain before returning us to the Eastern seaboard. We were married very young, and so in the early years, when the holidays came around and we found ourselves and our young children in unfamiliar places, we were very unsure of ourselves in our new roles as "patriarch" and "matriarch." Wherever we were, however, there was a Jewish community that took us in, found us places at Seder tables, told us where to buy *matzot* in Buenos Aires (where Pesah comes in the autumn, and all the years of conditioning of Pesah as a spring holiday have to be forgotten and only the more abstract—and therefore more real —meaning of the holiday is remembered), and distributed Hanukkah candles and *dreydlach* [small tops] which had come from the Jewish Welfare Board. When we finally settled in Princeton, New Jersey, one of the first things we did was to join the Jewish Center. For years we had been on the receiving end of Jewish communities around the world, and they had seemed actually grateful to us for having provided opportunities to give. In a curious and beautiful way we were the catalysts for the *mitzvot* of others. Now, with maturing children of our own, it was our turn to become part of the structure of a community which, just by *being*, does so much.

A synagogue is different things to different people; it is meant to be. For all of us it is to some degree an extension of ourselves and our homes, and as such it is another place we can enhance with needlework. Many of the projects found in other sections of this book could be made for the synagogue as well as for the home, but I would like to present some projects especially for synagogue use. They are meant to be worked by groups, in accordance with the spirit of community.

Torah mantle

The exact origins of the synagogue as an institution are obscure. Scholars, however, generally maintain that houses of prayer and religious instruction existed in the Land of Israel as well as in the Diaspora for at least several centuries before the destruction of the Second Temple. The major function of the synagogue is that of a house for worship and learning, even while it fulfills social and recreational needs in contemporary life. The Torah scroll is the most important and sacred object in the synagogue. The mantle that covers the Torah, the ark that houses it, and the table from which it is read can all be embellished with needlework.

Synagogues usually have more than one Torah, and their mantles are changed for the various holidays, or seasonally, or

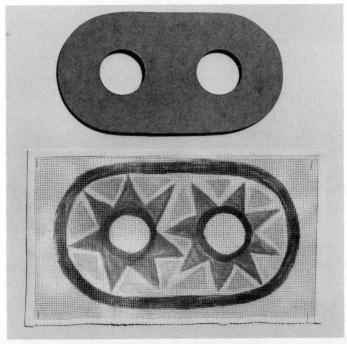

FIGURE 106: Design for a needlepoint Torah mantle painted on three sections of canvas. (Courtesy: Bogdonoff family, Temple Shalom, Matawan, N.J.)

both if there are enough covers. A worthwhile and exciting undertaking for a needlework group would be to make several varied Torah mantles for their synagogue. Though it appears complicated, the actual construction of a Torah mantle is quite simple. It can be made with one large piece of fabric seamed in the back, which is then attached to an oval top with holes in it to fit over the staves. Or, to allow more people to work on it, the main section can be divided in half and then seamed on both sides. Anyone familiar with simple dressmaking could assemble it or (especially when very heavy fabrics are used) an upholsterer could put it together.

A Torah cover or mantle can be made of any fabric that is strong enough to withstand the amount of wear it will receive. Velvet has often been used and, being so closely woven, is extremely durable; but precisely because it has been used so much, it seems like a cliché before you even begin. There are many beautiful wools and synthetics available now that would serve well in contemporary synagogues. Canvas embroidery, with its infinite possibilities of color, stitch, and pattern, offers a challenging way to make a Torah cover. The leftover yarn can be used on a scrap of canvas to make a coordinated Torah binder.

Sometimes a family, to commemorate a significant personal event—a birth, recovery from illness, a *bar mitzvah*, or a marriage—will donate some special article to the synagogue. The design of the Torah cover shown here was commissioned by a New Jersey family in honor of the forthcoming *bat mitzvah* of their youngest daughter. Over the next year or so, the canvas will be embroidered by the mother and her friends; hopefully, it will be completed and presented to the synagogue on the occasion of the *bat mitzvah*. The family was especially intrigued with the phrase from Deuteronomy 8:8—"a land of wheat and barley, and vines and fig-trees and pomegranates; a land of olive-trees and honey"—and wanted to incorporate this pastoral imagery into their Torah cover. The design was developed by the paper-cut method described earlier, then painted on No. 10 canvas with diluted acrylic paints. The work will be carried out in basketweave tent stitch using closely related earth tones of Persian wool. Details such as leaf veins will be reembroidered over the completed canvas.

The *parokhet*

The *parokhet* (ark curtain) has its origin in the curtain of the desert sanctuary, which was hung "between the holy place and the most holy" (Exodus 26:33). The curtain of "blue, and purple, and scarlet, and fine twined linen" was patterned with cherubim (Exodus 26:31).

The traditional *parokhet* we see in museums is usually a rectangle of heavily embroidered silk or velvet. While the construction is simple, the design is usually ornate. Contemporary synagogues often have sculpturally formed arks or elaborate systems for opening and closing the curtain. These require that each ark curtain be designed specifically for the ark it is to cover.

While a community group could do the actual needlework, it is a good idea to work closely with the building's architect or with a professional artist-designer if your synagogue ark requires anything other than a simple rectangular curtain. Robert Motherwell, Helen Frankenthaler, and Adolph Gottlieb are among well-known contemporary artists who have designed ark curtains.

The *hupah*

There is a story (reputed to be close to two thousand years old) of a cynic who sneeringly asked the Rabbi: "This God of yours, after the first six days of labor creating the world, what has He been doing?" To which the Rabbi replied: "Arranging marriages." A talmudic comment is that the perfect marriage occurs as frequently as the parting of the Red Sea. Whichever way you look at it, according to Jewish tradition the first questions we will be asked on Judgment Day are "Have you married?" "Have you founded a family?" The Jewish concept of marriage and family has always been a moral and sacred one. Each couple is seen as a new Adam and Eve standing again at the beginning of time in a new Garden of Eden.

Unfortunately, the wedding ceremonies we see portrayed in the mass media, and come to think of as typical of all marriage ceremonies, have nothing of the warmth, beauty, and symbolism of a Jewish wedding. Movies, television, and magazine advertising tell us that the bride is "given away" by her father, or some other male relation, to the groom, who has been mysteriously placed at the end of a long aisle. In a Jewish wedding, the bride and groom are each brought to the *hupah* [wedding canopy] by *both* their parents, who stand nearby during the service.

The *hupah*, basically a piece of fabric fastened at the corners to four poles, is usually held by friends of the couple, although sometimes stationary canopies are used. Some synagogues use elaborate floral bowers to simulate a *hupah;* others simply stretch a *tallit* between the supporting poles. The idea of using a bridal canopy probably goes back to the tent or chamber of the bridegroom in which the marriage was consummated (Joel 2:16, Psalm 19:5–6). Today the *hupah* symbolizes the new

FIGURE 107: Appliqué and embroidery *hupah*

home that the couple is about to establish. The *hupah* is often decorated with stars and moons, signifying that the marriage takes place with heavenly sanction.

The *hupah* shown here was made for the synagogue of the Rutgers University Hillel Foundation. Between weddings, it hangs on the synagogue wall as a banner. Holes were made in the four corners of the *hupah* and reinforced with shower-curtain grommets. These holes allow the decorative wooden finials to screw into the supporting poles. Poles and finials were purchased in a drapery shop. When the *hupah* is in use, the loops at either end serve as decorative fringes. The *hupah* was designed so that it could be hung from either end by threading a short drapery rod through the loops and hanging the rod from wall brackets.

One could also make a *hupah* for an individual couple, which could be hung in their new home after the ceremony or made into a bed canopy. A *hupah* made and presented by the bridesmaids would surely be cherished for life. It is a very gratifying project to work on because it brings out the natural optimism and sentimentality of everyone who is associated with it. Any technique or fabric can be used, and the project could be made by an individual or a group. I chose to do this *hupah* in appliqué and free embroidery (cotton fabrics on a woolen ground) because that approach contributed to the lighthearted feeling of the thematic material of birds and flowers interwoven with the phrase "voice of joy and voice of gladness" קול ששון וקול שמחה.   This is part of the seven benedictions recited after the bridegroom has placed a ring on the finger of the bride. These seven blessings are represented on the appliqué *hupah* as seven birds, some of which are crowned to indicate their relationship with the Divine.

The seven blessings beautifully illustrate how all of the ordinary events in human life are, in the Jewish tradition, linked to the mystical and historical life of Israel as a people. The seventh blessing is: "Praised are You, O Lord our God, King of the universe, who created joy and gladness, bride and groom, mirth, song, delight and rejoicing, love and harmony, peace and companionship. O Lord our God, may there be heard in the cities of Judah and in the streets of Jerusalem voices of joy and gladness, voices of bride and groom, and jubilant voices of those joined in marriage under the bridal canopy, the voices of young people feasting and singing. Praised are You, O Lord, who causes the groom to rejoice with his bride."

Some Ornaments
for the Jewish Home

We cannot make [God] visible to us, but we can make
ourselves visible to Him.

> Abraham J. Heschel *

UNLESS WE PUT things on the wall merely to cover cracks in
the plaster, whatever we put there for decorative reasons should
in some way embody aspects of life that we value most deeply.
Our minds and hearts are reflected on our walls. Not that
everything need be fraught with profound messages—art can
be funny or purely aesthetic. But ornaments should do more
than match sofas and rugs. The following objects were designed
to be as decorative as possible, yet all serve a spiritual or educational function as well.

When the gentile prophet Balaam said, "How goodly are
thy tents, O Jacob, Thy dwellings, O Israel" (Numbers 24:5),
he meant more than that Jewish homes had good interior deco-
rators. This saying of Balaam, whose intention was to curse
Israel but who ended up singing its praises, suggests a Jewish
home with the qualities of a sanctuary. Of course, the spiritual
and the aesthetic are often interdependent. How a home *feels*
has a lot to do with how it *looks*. Since home is where children
are made into *mentshen* [people], what they see around them
—in their rooms and throughout the house—should be instructive at the same time that it is aesthetically and morally up-
lifting.

* *Man's Quest for God: Studies in Prayer and Symbolism* (New York,
1954), p. 5.

The *mezuzah*

The first of the wall projects given here is usually the first thing one sees on coming into a Jewish home: a *mezuzah*. Usually the small parchment scroll containing the two scriptural passages of Deuteronomy 6:4–9 and 11:13–21 is rolled and placed in a small capsule. The capsule has a window in it, through which can be seen the inscription שדי [Shaddai, one of the names for God].

These two passages, plus Numbers 15:37–41, are collectively called the *Shema*. This prayer, which begins with the words "Hear O Israel, the Lord our God, the Lord is One," is said daily upon awakening in the morning and before retiring, and has often been the last words of Jewish martyrs who have died for the Sanctification of the Name. The *Shema* declares the unity of the One God and our desire and duty to live our lives with a spirit of dedication. Affixing these scriptural passages at the entrance to every room set aside for human activities is a reminder to whoever enters and leaves that the place is a Jewish home devoted to the ideals of service to God and mankind which are taught in the Torah.

Other nations have inscribed their creed on huge monuments of stone. With the centuries, their meanings were lost and the stones were used to build newer edifices or were covered by the accumulated débris of time. The *mezuzah*, a tiny handwritten piece of parchment, affixed anew at each Jewish home, and periodically checked to make certain that it has not become blurred, mildewed, or torn, has survived as tenaciously as the Jewish people itself.

The capsule form originated in ancient days when a reed was used to protect the parchment against becoming torn and

FIGURE 108: *Mezuzah* before being assembled

FIGURE 109: Detail of the border of the *mezuzah*

dirty. Many beautiful, cylindrical *mezuzah* containers have been and continue to be made in a variety of materials including silver, wood, and porcelain. The cylindrical form is well suited to an ordinary doorpost (in fact, the word *mezuzah* literally means doorpost), but in much of contemporary architecture there are not always suitable doorposts at entries to rooms. Though usually supported internally by post-and-lintel construction, entries are often broad passages through which one room flows into another. In these cases a small *mezuzah* tube looks insignificant and, unfortunately, is often omitted altogether. The following project will hopefully be appropriate to the architectural characteristics of such homes.

Nothing should be added to the scriptural verses in the *mezuzah*, but the outside container can be made to go with any style of home decor. I prefer a container in which the actual parchment can be seen, since it is the words, after all, that are most significant and about which the container should be designed to remind us.

In the following design, the *mezuzah* parchment is flat and the container is a new type of plastic frame generally available at photo, hobby, and art-supply stores as well as department stores. A traditional frame can also be used; in that case, you would be using the side panels as a border. Or omit them altogether. Since the overall size is small, you might splurge on

FIGURE 110: The *mezuzah* with its plastic box-frame

FIGURE 111: Pattern for the wheeled ark

an elaborate molding. If handwritten parchment scrolls are not available through your synagogue gift shop, they can be ordered by mail.

The embroidery, which is done in simple stitches in shades of gold and yellow on a dark brown cotton fabric background, encloses the parchment in a Torah ark which is set on wheels. The original ark built in the wilderness was transported by means of long poles through rings in the manner of a litter or stretcher. As the Jews moved about, however, subsequent Torah arks were mounted on wheels. In the ruins of the second-to-fourth–century synagogue at Capernaum, on the shores of the Galilee, there is a stone frieze with a carving of an ark in the style of a miniature Greek temple on wheels. The murals in the third-century Dura Europos synagogue in western Syria also show a wheeled ark. In an age of freight trains, moving vans, and air transport, it is perhaps archaic to use such a simple caravanlike form, but its simplicity symbolizes for me the centuries of wanderings of the Jewish people, with the Torah as our spiritual guide.

The birds on top of the ark are for ornamental purposes. However, for me they might be the legendary phoenix who, according to the Talmud, was allowed to stay in the Garden of Eden after the banishment of Adam and Eve as a reward for his attempt to keep them from eating the forbidden fruit.

The drawing for the central part of the *mezuzah* is given full-size. Extend the border design to fill the 7″ horizontal measurement, and repeat it for the side panels.

MATERIALS:
fabric rectangle 11″ x 9″, to be trimmed after completion to 9½″ x 7½″
embroidery or cotton pearl thread in an assortment of shades of the color of your background fabric

I used brown fabric, with tones of gold and copper. This was done so the parchment would be the brightest spot in the design. You could work the design in any combination of colors.

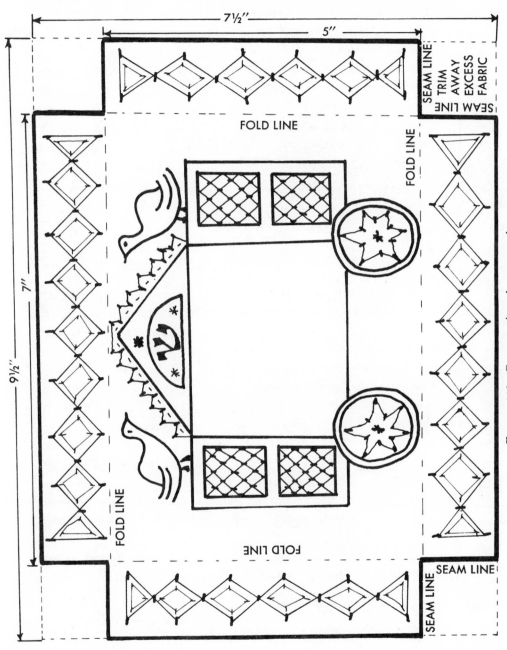

FIGURE 112: Constructing the *mezuzah*

7½″

5″

SEAM LINE

TRIM AWAY EXCESS FABRIC

SEAM LINE

FOLD LINE

FOLD LINE

7″

9½″

FOLD LINE

FOLD LINE

SEAM LINE

SEAM LINE

STITCHES:

Outline stitch for the birds and the ark
Lattice laid-and-couched for the doors on the ark
Buttonhole stitch as the wheels
Threaded running stitches for the borders and as the zigzag along the top of the ark, and for the wheel spokes

After the embroidery is completed, seam the corner notch closed, forming a boxlike shape (Fig. 112). Slip this over the cardboard form that comes with the frame. Carefully lay the parchment in place and enclose all in the plastic cover.

The *mizrah*

Another uniquely Jewish wall ornament suitable for any room in the house is a special marker for the eastern wall which is known as a *mizrah*. The word *mizrah*, which originally meant "rising of the sun," now means "east." In the days of the Temple, Jews in prayer there faced the Holy of Holies. Elsewhere in Jerusalem, they turned toward the Temple. Outside of Jerusalem, they faced the Holy City. In our exile the custom grew up of marking the wall that faced east, the direction where the Temple once stood. Sometimes this was accomplished by omitting a stone or some plaster, but soon more decorative techniques were used to add beauty to holiness. *Mizrahim* have been made as paper-cuts, watercolors, and oil paintings. They have also been made of wood, brass, silver, enamel, and plastic.

Just about any of the motifs in this book, worked in any technique, would be suitable for a *mizrah*. If just the word "*mizrah*" is desired, the crenellated *alef-bet* (see Appendix) would offer an attractive and suitable form. Colors can be chosen to harmonize or contrast with those of the rest of the room.

FIGURE 113: Needlepoint *mizrah*. Some of the foliage and the tablets are not visible in this photograph; for the details, see Plate X

FIGURE 114: Crewel *mizrah*

Mizrahim can also go in children's rooms. You could explain the purpose of the *mizrah* to the child and let him do the drawing for you. The two designs given here use an assortment of symbols to turn our thoughts toward Jerusalem, our Holy City.

SYMBOLS IN THE NEEDLEPOINT AND CREWEL MIZRAHIM

Pillars and Pomegranates

According to a story I heard as a child, when Solomon was building his Temple he called on help from every possible source, even from demons. As he was directing the placement of the pillars in front of the Temple, a demon appeared and said that if Solomon would grant them permission, he and his associate, the demon of the Red Sea, would bring the most beautiful pillar in the world, which rested at the bottom of the Red Sea, and erect it in front of the Temple. Solomon, eager to have the most beautiful of everything in the Temple, agreed. Later, when he saw the demons flying through the air carrying a glorious pillar which glistened and shone and stretched the full length of the sky, he realized that they intended to drop it on him and destroy not only him but the Temple and the world as well. King Solomon drew a circle in the air with his magic ring and commanded the demons to stop and never leave the sky or their pillar. On clear nights you can still see the pillar, which some call the Milky Way.

Solomon the Wise settled for two copper pillars decorated with pomegranates to place at the right and left of the Temple porch. Pillars and pomegranates originally were fertility symbols (though the rabbis have often interpreted the pillars as representing the columns of fire and cloud which accompanied the Israelites in the wilderness). But as is the case with all symbols adopted from surrounding cultures by the Hebrews, the forms remained the same while their inner meanings changed.

Thus the pomegranate came to symbolize life and Torah (the Hebrew word for pomegranates, *rimmonim,* is also the word for the ornamental finials of the Torah scroll rods), while the pillars came to be identified with a longing for the return to Zion. The Temple pillars are a common motif for *mizrahim.*

Cherubim

The cherubim first made their appearance in Jewish art in the Tent of Meeting made to God's specifications by the Hebrews in the wilderness. Exodus 25:18 ff. tells us that huge (six feet at least) golden cherubim were placed at either end of the ark cover. They faced each other with their wings spread. They represented God's nearness to humanity, for He promised to speak from "between the two cherubim" (Exodus 25:22). The veil separating the most sacred part of the Tabernacle from the rest of the tent was also ornamented with cherubim, which the eleventh-century biblical commentator Rashi says were woven directly into the fabric.

Contemporary scholars identify the cherub with the Egyptian winged sphinx, which had the body of a lion and a human face. But the Talmud reached the popular imagination first with the conception of cherubim with the chubby faces and bodies of children. The childlike cherub became so popular in Christian art that it was discarded by many for use in Jewish objects, although it continued to appear from time to time. The lion, and sometimes other beasts, became its replacement, as a decorative, symbolic honor guard for the Tablets of the Law and the Ark. It is ironic that Jews have often abandoned biblical symbols when Christianity adopted them, allowing, as it were, Christians to appropriate these symbols as their own and coming to regard them as Christian and "un-Jewish."

The Tree of Life

For both *mizrahim,* I have used the Tree of Life as a motif. The concept of the Tree of Life is so ancient and so complex and still somehow so powerful that to simply use an ordinary tree to represent this idea is inadequate. Imagine a time when the largest thing around (aside from mountains) is a tree. It outlives humans, so perhaps it is immortal. It draws its sustenance from the depths of the earth and the far reaches of the sky. In our day, we have limited the grandeur of trees by our capacity to build higher than them and to string telephone wires through them. We are beginning to see that we have lost something in the process.

All of our troubles seem to have begun by violating a tree. Lest Adam and Eve should gain immortality by eating from the Tree of Life after they had already eaten from the Tree of Knowledge, they were driven from the Garden of Eden, and cherubim with flaming swords were set at the entrance to the garden to protect the Tree of Life (Genesis 3:23–24).

The rods upon which the Torah scrolls are rolled are called Trees of Life. And the Torah itself, which nourishes the mind and the spirit and is eternal, "is a Tree of Life to them that lay hold upon her" (Proverbs 3:18).

On the crewel embroidery a pair of *menorot* support and are supported by a Tree of Life in the form of a vine. Growing from the vine are grapes, pomegranates, and olive leaves—three of the seven ancient fruits of Israel—as well as ornamental flowers.

The stylized tree used for the design of the needlepoint *mizrah* is based on sacred trees carved on several ninth-century B.C.E. Assyrian marble panels. I have used a total of seven foliage forms, as well as seven petals within each form, to signify the connection between the seven-branched *menorah* and the Tree of Life to which the *menorah* is related.

The Menorah

Since antiquity, the *menorah* has been the single most important and authentic Jewish symbol. Its strength lies in its combination of earthly and heavenly forces. Its form is basically that of a tree with a central branch and six additional branches which terminate at the same height as the central branch. These seven branches bear light as their fruit. It is said that the seven lamps represent the seven days of Creation, with the central flame representing the Sabbath.

The seven planets of the ancient world were the moon and the sun (which we know today are not planets at all), Mars, Saturn, Venus, Mercury, and Jupiter. The seven lamps of the *menorah* are identified with "these seven, which are the eyes of the Lord, that run to and fro through the whole earth" (Zechariah 4:10). The flames thus represent the divine, and the treelike *menorah* becomes a powerful, abstract emblem of life and light.

The first *menorah* was made by the divinely inspired Bezalel from a solid block of gold for the tent of worship in the desert (Exodus 37:17 ff.) and was later brought to Solomon's Temple. There were ten additional candelabra in Solomon's Temple as well. The single *menorah* in the Second, or Herod's, Temple was probably a reconstruction made according to its description in the Bible. When this Second Temple was destroyed in 70 C.E. by the Romans, all of the Temple furnishings disappeared. The Arch of Titus in Rome shows the *menorah* and other spoils from Jerusalem being carried away by the Romans. Because this is an arch celebrating the victory of Imperial Rome over the Jews, Jews even today will not knowingly walk under it so as to avoid symbolic participation in that terrible, triumphal parade.

For centuries people have fantasized about the possible whereabouts of the Temple *menorah*.* According to talmudic legend, this speculation is unnecessary since all the Temple furnishings including the *menorah* went up in flames when the Temple was destroyed and will descend again in flames when the Messiah comes.

---

* For example, Nathaniel Hawthorne, in his novel *The Marble Faun*, theorizes that the *menorah* is buried in the mud of the river Tiber in Rome, and has one of his characters say, "Such a candlestick cannot be lost forever. When it is found again, and seven lights are kindled and burning in it, the whole world will gain the illumination it needs."

Many people confuse the *hanukkiah* [the nine-branched lamp used at Hanukkah] with the *menorah*. This is a natural mistake, since, beginning in the twelfth century, Hanukkah lamps were often made in the *menorah* form even though the seven-branched *menorah* was not in ritual use. The more typical form for a Hanukkah lamp was that of a low "bench" with eight lamps in front of a flat vertical background which holds the ninth lamp. Hanukkah lamps either stood or were hung on the wall.

Doves

Doves are very common in Jewish art. I have used them for several other projects in this book besides the crewel *mizrah*. After the Flood, Noah sent a dove out of the ark to see if there was any dry land. The bird returned with an olive branch in its beak, and the dove with an olive branch has been a symbol of peace and tranquility ever since. The dove, like the fish, was a symbol of fertility and, because of its nesting habits, is associated with domesticity. The dove is used to represent Israel throughout the Bible. The *Shekhinah* (the Divine Presence) is often symbolized by a white dove. Doves nest in the Western Wall in Jerusalem, and no one would think of driving them away.

Crowns

Rabbi Simeon ben Yohai (ca. 100–160) said, "There are three crowns; the crown of learning, the crown of priesthood, and the crown of royalty; but the crown of a good name excels them all" (Pirke Abot IV, 17). Crowns appear with great frequency as a decorative motif in Jewish art, especially as symbolic of the dignity and majesty of the Law and of learning. The scrolls of the Law in the synagogue are often ornamented with elaborate silver crowns into which fit the tops of the rollers. A midrashic legend speaks of angels collecting all the prayers and words of praise and weaving them into a crown for the King of the Universe.

NEEDLEPOINT MIZRAH

FINISHED SIZE: 12½″ x 19½″

MATERIALS:
No. 10 cotton mono canvas, 18″ x 25″. The design can also be worked on a finer mesh (higher number), for clearer definition of the curves if desired
Background: 3½ oz. light gold-green wool
Pillar, corner ornaments, leaf centers, stars on Tablets: 1 oz. deep red
Branches and topmost leaf: 1 oz. dark olive green
Tree trunk: ½ oz. dark brown
Outline and bands on tree: 6 feet (one strand) black
Cherubim and letters: 1 oz. white
Tablets, remaining leaves, and features of cherubim: 1 oz. gold

Make drawings of two cherubim facing in opposite directions. To make the mirror-image pattern, place a piece of carbon paper face up on the table with a new sheet of paper over that. Place your first cherub drawing over this and redraw the lines. With the carbon paper on the bottom rather than in the middle, you will get a reverse image of the design.

For the Tree of Life, fold a 16″-long piece of the tracing paper in half lengthwise. Place the fold against the dotted center line and draw half of the tree. Repeat the trunk with its foliage two more times for one-half of the complete tree. By using the carbon-paper method described above with the rolled-under half of the tracing paper, you will have the complete tree.

Draw the Tablets and corner ornaments on small pieces of paper.

Arrange the drawings on a large sheet of paper as shown (Fig. 113) and draw the pillars with the aid of a ruler. The letters מזרח [*mizrah*] are in the cross stitch *alef-bet* in the Appendix.

FIGURE 115: Pattern for the cherub with tablet

CORNER ORNAMENT

REPEAT FROM

CENTER LINE

FIGURE 116: Pattern for the Tree of Life

10 STITCHES = 1"

Figure 117: Pattern for the needlepoint *mizrah*

Glue the pieces in place securely. Make certain that all the lines are dark enough to be visible through the canvas. Tape drawing to a table to keep it from moving. Center the canvas over the design and also secure the corners with tape. Using indelible felt-tip pens, India ink, or acrylic paint, draw the design on the canvas, using the tracings underneath as your guide. Use colors that are either the same as or lighter than the design, because sometimes the canvas can show through.

This *mizrah* was worked almost entirely in the basketweave tent stitch. The only exceptions are the pillars which were done in brick stitch. This was to give them additional texture, suggesting the hammered copper pillars, called Boaz and Jakhin, on the porch of Solomon's Temple. After the Tablets were completed in tent stitch, they were reembroidered with a double cross stitch.

When the needlepoint is completed and blocked, fold under 1″ of the 2″–3″ of unworked canvas surrounding the design and stitch securely by hand or machine. Cut a piece of corrugated cardboard the same size as the worked area of the canvas. Place the needlepoint face down on a table and put the cardboard on top of it. Fold the excess canvas around the cardboard. Miter the corners. Use straight pins to secure the canvas to the cardboard.

Thread your tapestry needle with strong cord and tightly lace the surplus canvas across the back of the cardboard, as indicated in the diagram. Begin lacing at the center and go back

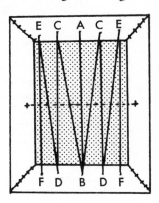

FIGURE 118: Mounting

and forth at 1″ intervals. Do the vertical lacing first, then repeat the procedure for the horizontal lacing. If it does not seem taut enough, add another row of lacing between the 1″ intervals.

CREWEL EMBROIDERED MIZRAH

Crewel embroidery is usually done with fine woolen yarn on a linen background. In fact, the word "crewel" refers to the type of yarn rather than to the style of embroidery. As was mentioned earlier, Mosaic law prohibits the mixture of fibers of linen with those of wool. This prohibition, however, applies only to clothing or to something that might conceivably be used for warmth. Since this *mizrah* cannot in any way be worn, it is permissible to make it using linen fabric embroidered with woolen crewel yarn. If, however, this makes you uncomfortable, a different fabric could be used for the background material (cotton, synthetic, or sheer wool) or the embroidery could be done with embroidery floss or cotton pearl thread.

The finished *mizrah* shown measures 17″ x 22″ (not including the additional fabric around the design to fill out the secondhand frame). One-fourth of the design is given full-size. It can be made this size, with a resulting embroidery of 8½″ x 11″, or enlarged to whatever size you desire.

Draw the design on a large sheet of paper first and then transfer it to the fabric, using dressmaker's tracing paper. If you are using linen, press very hard as you transfer the design, since the texture of the fabric makes it resist accurate drawing. Spray with fixative.

Crewel thread is sold in distinctive small packages. I have indicated below the number of such packages you will need. The suggested amount is generous to allow for mistakes and practice stitches. Two strands of thread are used throughout except when indicated otherwise.

EACH SQUARE = 1″

FIGURE 119: Pattern for crewel *mizrah*, with grid

COLOR AND QUANTITY	OBJECT	STITCH
brown, 3	branches	average of 5 rows of outline stitch, single strand
	birds' eyes grape stems	2 lines of outline stitch, single thread
purple, 1	grapes	satin
white, 2	doves	laid-and-couched: couching in beige
	crown	laid-and-couched: diagonal in gold, securing stitches in dark red cross stitch
	letters	satin
beige, 1	doves	outline with single strand, couching of white cross threads
dark red, 1	pomegranates	long and short, outline
	flowers	satin
	crown	small cross stitch to couch gold diagonals
	flame center	lazy daisy
light red, 1	pomegranates	long and short
	flowers	satin
	letters	satin stitch circles
light gold, 1	flames	chain
	birds' feet and beaks	outline
	crown	outline, single strand
dark gold, 2	*menorah*	chain, 4 rows average
	crown	diagonal couched lines, single strand
	letters	outline
light brown, 1	*menorah* outline	chain stitch
dark green, 2	tendrils	outline with single strand, average 4–5 rows
	pomegranate leaves	satin stitch, single strand
	⅓ other leaves	closed fishbone
medium green, 1	⅓ leaves	closed fishbone
light green, 1	⅓ leaves	closed fishbone

Do the embroidery on fabric that is at least 3″ larger all around than the finished size you desire. When the embroidery is complete, place it face down on an ironing board which has been well padded with toweling and iron it with a steam iron or using a damp cloth. Padding the board will keep the embroidery in relief rather than letting it be pressed flat under the weight of the iron. Stretch it over cardboard, following the directions that accompany the needlepoint *mizrah*.

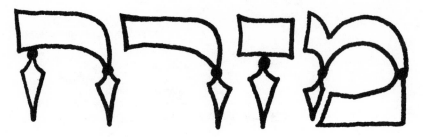

FIGURE 120: Letters for crewel *mizrah*

FELT APPLIQUÉ FRAME

When I walked into my twelve-year-old son's room and saw the certificate he had received from our synagogue when he began going to religious school classes several years back taped to the wall over his desk, I was shamed into giving it the proper attention it deserves. I'm sure every family has an assortment of meaningful documents which could be decoratively framed and hung—naming certificates, wedding announcements, confirmation diplomas, and marriage contracts, to mention a few of the possibilities.

The Jewish *ketubah* [wedding contract] was traditionally richly embellished. Today, unfortunately, most of them are machine printed and are not often particularly interesting. By making a special mat for it and having it suitably framed, even the simplest *ketubah*, now folded away in a drawer, can at least be somewhat enhanced.

FIGURE 121: Felt appliqué frame

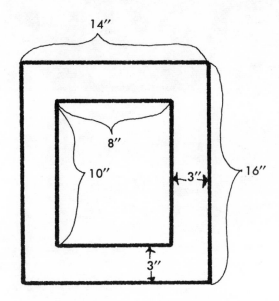

FIGURE 122: Measurements for the frame

I designed this mat by making a paper-cut using a few simple symbols. The paper-cut then became the pattern from which the white felt was cut. No hemming is necessary with felt. The cut-out shapes were pinned in place and sewn to the background with cotton pearl. I used a combination of blind stitches and running stitches with an occasional lazy daisy stitch and double cross stitch for embellishment. The *menorah* was chain-stitched. Felt has a tendency to stretch, so be sure to pin very carefully. Do not cut out the center opening until all the sewing is done.

This design could also be used for a needlepoint frame, using a fine canvas. Or it could be embroidered in bright colors on a contrasting background. It is suitable for a mirror or for photographs. The measurements can be easily changed by adjusting the length of the vines.

INNER EDGE OF MAT

FIGURE 123: Patterns for the frame

A L E F - B E T *S A M P L E R*

This embroidery was done using the traditional *alef-bet* (see Appendix, page 249). I omitted the final forms of the letters *khaf*, *mem*, *fe*, and *tzadi*. The dove was perched over the *het* to add a little variety. The colors I used were chosen to go with my daughter's quilt which I had started the year before, and now that both quilt and sampler are complete, they make up the dominant color and decoration of her room, which is otherwise basically white. The sampler was done on linen with cotton embroidery floss and was very pleasant to work, since each letter represents a satisfying accomplishment. I decided the colors first and planned their distribution on a scrap of paper. I made up or learned the stitches as I embroidered each letter, trying for a balance between the densely filled letters and the more airy ones. Linen is very pleasant to work on—though I never use it for things that are washed frequently, because I hate to iron—and I enjoy using it for framed pieces. I worked on a large piece of fabric and then trimmed the finished embroidery to fit the junkshop frame, which measures 15½″ x 20″.

FIGURE 124: *Alef-bet* sampler

FIGURE 125: Pattern for dove

The same *alef-bet* was used by a friend to make a pair of pillows for her sons' room. She used many shades of gold on a red background and a variety of stitches.

CHAYA FAIGLE'S APPLIQUÉ: TWO BOYS SMOKING PIPES

I mentioned earlier that my grandmother sewed. My great-grandmother did also. Together, they made the trousseaus for many of the girls of their Polish town. My great-grandmother would sew, supervising a group of helpers, and my grandmother did the designs. These were drawn on paper and then sewn through the paper onto the fabric. The paper was ripped away when the sewing was completed. When my mother came to this country in 1923, she brought with her a trunkful of embroidered petticoats, nightgowns, and table linens. She sent most of these objects back to Poland, because only machine-made things were considered fashionable here then.

My grandmother sent the appliqué shown here to my mother in the early 1930's. I present this to you because many people enjoy working "heritage" designs (Colonial Williamsburg and the like). So I am sharing my *"shtetl* heritage" with you. My grandmother had no need to add obvious Jewish symbols or letters to the embroidery of the boys: they lived and played in a totally Jewish environment. They are naturally wearing *yarmulkas.* Just a few short years after the appliqué of the boys came to the United States, the thousand-year-old Polish-Jewish culture of which it was a part was destroyed. Since my grandmother's tombstone is only a wisp of cloud (as in Elie Wiesel's image in *Gates of the Forest*), perhaps sharing her embroidery will, in part, memorialize her life.

APPLIQUÉ AND EMBROIDERY FINISHED SIZE: 15" x 23"

MATERIALS:
linen for background, assorted fabric scraps for clothes (some velvet is nice)
embroidery thread: black for legs, arms, faces, and hair; colors to go with the fabrics you use for the others

Figure 126: Chaya Faigle's appliqué: two boys smoking pipes

Enlarge the drawings of the boys and dog either by the grid method or have it done photographically. Make patterns from cardboard for the clothing shapes by placing carbon paper under the enlarged drawing and redrawing it. Or use tracing paper instead of cardboard if you prefer to have transparent paper patterns. Use the enlarged drawing with dressmaker's tracing paper to put the lines for embroidery on your fabric, using the photograph as a guide in placing the figures. Spray lightly with fixative.

Cut the fabric into the shapes of the clothes and pin in place. For better composition, repeat one or two of the colors in the clothes of both boys. In my grandmother's design, one boy has a red shirt and the other a red *yarmulka*. One boy's socks are blue (very faded now); the other has blue shorts. My grandmother did not turn under the edges of the appliquéd fabric since she used heavy, closely woven materials. She stitched the clothing pieces on with small close buttonhole stitches. The cuffs of the socks and edges of the caps were done in satin stitch. I don't know what kind of thread she used, but it looks like three strands of embroidery floss for some of it and fine cotton pearl (or silk buttonhole twist) for other parts. Outline stitch was used for all the linear work.

FIGURE 127: Design for two boys smoking pipes, with grid

EACH SQUARE = 1″

FIGURE 128: Detail: boy with ball

FIGURE 129: Detail: boy with dog

TWO BOYS ON A TRICYCLE APPLIQUÉ

FIGURE 130: The photograph of my husband's father and brother, the basis for the appliqué

FIGURE 131: Two boys on a tricycle appliqué

My husband's father grew up in New York City, where his immigrant parents had a candy store. This photograph was taken in front of that store in 1909. My father-in-law is seated on the tricycle with his younger brother, Abe, behind him. A few years ago Uncle Abe died. When his daughter, our cousin, had her first baby shortly after, she named him for her father. As a birthday gift to the baby, I made the appliqué shown here. It was inspired by my grandmother's appliqué, but I used the photograph of the two brothers in their sailor suits as my model. The Hebrew phrase surrounding them is from Psalm 133 and says: "Behold, how good and how pleasant it is for brethren to dwell together in unity!"

הנה מה טוב ומה נעים שבת אחים גם יחד

Look through your family photographs and you will most likely find an intriguing old one that is adaptable to appliqué or embroidery. Or why not use a recent backyard snapshot of your growing children or grandchildren? They are fit subject matter for "heirlooms," since they will eventually receive them. Select a photograph that has simple and well-defined shapes. Draw your patterns freehand from the picture if it is simple enough, or have the photograph blown up at a photo-processing shop that does work for architects, if one is available in your locality, rather than at a portrait studio which will charge you much more. If the original photograph is the right size, you might simply make several Xerox copies of it. You will need two copies of the drawings: one as a pattern and guide for the layout and the other to be cut apart and used as patterns for the various elements in the design (i.e., limbs, boys, and clothes) which are cut out of fabric and appliquéd.

SIMHAT TORAH APPLIQUÉ FLAGS AND BANNERS

The last project in the book is a collection of appliqué flags and banners. They can be easily made in an afternoon and would be a pleasant activity for a youth group. The motifs used have appeared in other incarnations earlier in the book.

Choose those you like the best, cut out letters for messages if you desire, and compose the shapes on a felt background. Other fabrics that do not ravel can be used along with felt. The stitching can be done by machine. However, I prefer simple running stitches, using a contrasting color either as an outline or to secure the shape with a few stitches down the center of it. Beads, buttons, bells, fringes, or other ornaments can be added for additional interest, amusement, and embellishment.

For a flag, have the design slightly off-center to allow enough fabric to fold over as a pocket along one edge to hold the wooden dowel. For a banner, fold the fabric at the top, or make loops in a contrasting fabric to hold the supporting rod. A vertical dowel, or strip of lattice, is tacked at the midpoint of the horizontal rod to provide a means of carrying the banner. It can also be hung from hooks on the wall.

The flags can be used as decorations for teenage or adult celebrations and hung on a wall later as a remembrance of the occasion. At the very least, a collection of them would be as interesting for a wall decoration as a group of athletic or college pennants. My intention, however, is to use them for Simhat Torah, the holiday of Rejoicing in the Law which culminates the autumn cycle of religious observance.

The Jewish New Year begins in the fall with Rosh Hashanah on the first and second days of Tishri (September–October). The following days are a period of reflection, meditation, and self-evaluation. It is a time to come to peace not

FIGURE 132: Five Simhat Torah flags and banners

only with God but with oneself and one's fellow human beings. The Ten Penitential Days end on Yom Kippur [the Day of Atonement], a fast day which is usually spent in solemn prayer in the synagogue. Upon return from the synagogue it is considered a *mitzvah* to begin construction of the temporary dwelling to be used during the joyful harvest festival of Sukkot, which begins five days after Yom Kippur and lasts for eight days. This holiday season is also called the Season of our Rejoicing. We rejoice in and give thanks for our many blessings: the harvest, our freedom, and, most of all, the Torah. The last day of this 23-day festive period is Simhat Torah. On that day the Torah scrolls are carried in joyful procession around the synagogue. Children join the parade holding miniature scrolls or flags, which are sometimes topped with apples. The apples, like the honey and other special foods enjoyed during the High Holy days period, symbolize a desire for a full, sweet New Year.

The Jews of the Soviet Union, whom Elie Weisel has called "the Jews of Silence," are denied the right to freely practice their religion or to emigrate to Israel. In recent years their situation has given new poignancy and intensity to Simhat Torah. On that one day of the year, tens of thousands of young and old people gather in the street around the great synagogue of Moscow and, knowing that there are government agents photographing them and noting their names, defy the authorities by singing and dancing into the night, thus affirming their faith and their Jewish identity in the very face of oppression.

Every Shabbat throughout the year, a section of the five books of the Bible is read. Amid the festivities (and often hilarity) of the Simhat Torah celebration, the last part of Deuteronomy and the first part of Genesis are read. This joining of the end to the beginning symbolizes the eternal in the word of God.

This book is only a beginning. I have tried to show that the Jewish heritage is rich in symbols and motifs which can inspire you to create your own delightful and profound needlework projects. For as Rabbi Tarfon is quoted as saying, "It is not your job to finish the work but you are not free to give up the task" (Pirke Abot II, 21).

FIGURE 133: Flag with cherubim and wheeled ark (actual size 18½" x 13½")

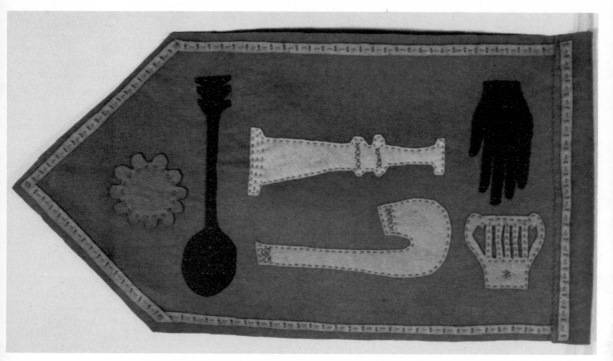

FIGURE 134: Flag with musical instruments (actual size 10½" x 20")

FIGURE 135: Flag with *menorah* (actual size 18" x 13")

FIGURE 136: Simhat Torah flag (actual size 14½″ x 17½″). The last letter of the last word ("Israel") in Deuteronomy, which completes the annual cycle of Torah reading, is a *lamed*. *Bet*, the initial of *"Bereshit"* ["In the beginning"], is the first letter of Genesis. Since on Simhat Torah the end and the beginning of the Pentateuch are read, *lamed* and *bet* are playfully combined to spell *"leb"* ["heart"]

FIGURE 137: Banner saying *"shalom"* (actual size 19½" x 22")

APPENDIX

THE ALEF-BET
AND HOW
TO USE IT

BASIC ALEF-BET

Nothing visual is so essentially Hebraic in character and feeling as the Hebrew alphabet, called in Hebrew the *alef-bet* from the names of the first two letters.* Each letter seems to have a personality of its own as well as a subtle familial relationship with its colleagues.

Hebrew is thought of as the holy tongue [*lashon hakodesh*] rather than simply a mother tongue. Legend recounts Moses, upon his arrival in heaven, finding God weaving crowns for the letters of the *alef-bet*, for the Universe was created through these letters.**

Today many American Jews, though probably the best secularly educated group in the world, are almost completely illiterate in Hebrew. Let us at least be like the humble cobbler in the hasidic tale who, raising his head to heaven, said: "Master of the Universe: what can I do? I want to pray to You properly but I have no time to study. I must work constantly for my bread and so unfortunately I know only the first ten letters of the *alef-bet*, and sometimes I'm not so sure which comes first, the *zayin* or the *het*. I'll tell You what, Master of the Universe, while I'm hammering on the shoes I'll recite the ten letters I know, and You, dear Lord, please arrange them in nice prayers to suit Yourself."

---

* We use the word "alphabet" so familiarly that we never pause to recognize its obvious connection to "*alef-bet*." The word "alphabet" is derived from the first two letters of Greek (*alpha* and *beta*), which are related to the Hebrew.

** Apparently the world is still being created through letters and numbers. We have so much faith in them that we have given over control of our lives to computers, even for choosing mates. Perhaps this "applied mathematics" is not very different after all from the practical numerology of the Kabbalists.

All European alphabets are derived from the same Semitic source as the Hebrew letters. With close scrutiny it is possible to see their common heredity. Often they appear as mirror images of the same basic form.

FIGURE 138: The letters *gimel*, *resh*, and *fe*, and their "mirror images" in the Roman alphabet

What makes them appear to differ more than they really do is the emphasis placed on the vertical line in the Roman alphabet and on the characteristic horizontal stroke, which grew out of the use of the quill, in the Hebrew. Hebrew letters are used for Yiddish, Ladino, and Aramaic as well as Hebrew.

FIGURE 139: The letters *gimel*, *resh*, and *fe* showing their emphasized horizontals, with the stronger verticals of the Roman alphabet

The Hebrew letters also have numerical value. Combinations of the letters are used in the Hebrew numbering system (as Roman letters make up Roman numerals) and in the Jewish calendar. The fact that the letters have a numerical value gave birth to an elaborate process whereby the numerical values of words are calculated and thereby additional meanings are read into a text. A simple, familiar example is that of the number 18 as a symbol of life. This is because the numerical sum of חי [life]—*het* (8) and *yod* (10)— equals 18. My sister was married in 1971, and since these four digits (1, 9, 7, 1) also total 18, the word חי was engraved on her wedding band. Many phrases can be played with like this even by the inexperienced, and one can come up with lovely ideas for inscriptions. Fifteen, for example, is the sum of the words "with love" in Hebrew באהבה and could be used for a fifteenth birthday, or an anniversary, or an occasion that falls on the fifteenth of the month.

The Hebrew alphabet is made up of twenty-two letters, all of which are consonants. Five of the letters have a different form when used at the end of the word: כך, מם, נן, פף, צץ. Five variants are created by placing a dot inside or above the letter: בב, כך, פפ, שׁשׂ, תת. Vowel sounds are indicated by the use of six signs made of dots and lines placed above, below, or in the center of the letter. The vowel signs are not used in the Scroll of the Law or in contemporary Hebrew newspapers and periodicals except in those intended for new immigrants to Israel learning Hebrew.

FIGURE 140: The Hebrew *Alef-Bet*

LETTER	NAME	SOUND	VALUE	LETTER	NAME	SOUND	VALUE
א	alef	silent	1	מ	mem	M	40
ב	bet	B	2	ם	final		
ב	vet	V			mem		
ג	gimel	G (get)	3	נ	nun	N	50
ד	dalet	D	4	ן	final		
ה	he	H	5		nun		
ו	vav	V	6	ס	samekh	S	60
ז	zayin	Z	7	ע	ayin	silent	70
ח	het	H (often		פ	pe	P	80
		translated		פ	fe	F	
		as Ch or		ף	final fe		
		Ḥ)	8	צ	tzadi	Tz	90
ט	tet	T	9	ץ	final		
י	yod	Y	10		tzadi		
כ	kaf	K	20	ק	kof	K	100
כ	khaf	kh		ר	resh	R	200
ך	final			שׁ	shin	Sh	300
	khaf			שׂ	sin	S	
ל	lamed	L	30	ת	tav	T	400

When transliterating English (or other foreign) names or words into Hebrew, you will need sounds that are not ordinarily used in Hebrew. The following system has been devised for putting foreign words into Hebrew characters. When a vowel is needed, use *alef* for A. Use *alef* and *yod* for I and E at the beginning of words. Use *yod* for Y when it sounds like the Y in "yellow" and for E and U in the middle of a word. Use *vav* for O in the middle of a word, and *alef* + *vav* for O at the beginning of a word. There is no J sound (as in Jennifer) or Ch (as in Charles) in Hebrew, so the practice has grown up of using accented letters for these sounds. The J is indicated by a *gimel* that has an accent mark over it ג׳ and the Ch with a similarly accented *tzadi* צ׳. W as in Wendy is indicated with two *vavim* וו. *Tav* is used for Th as in Theodore. Bringing ancient Hebrew into the modern world has given rise to many cross-lingual misspellings, so yours won't be the first. Remember, however, that Hebrew reads from right to left!

Syllables are traditionally not divided in Hebrew. In order to make all lines equal and have even margins on the page, six letters can be expanded horizontally. These are: *lamed, dalet, he, het, tav,* and *resh.*

FIGURE 141: Expanding letters horizontally

When planning a design using the *alef-bet*, remember to leave space for the ascending line of the *lamed* and the dropped verticals of the *kof* and the final *nun, pe, khaf,* and *tzadi*. This can be accomplished by leaving the space between the lines as wide as a letter is high. Another, more enjoyable, way— which takes more preplanning—is to juggle the lines a bit so the long verticals fit into empty spaces left in the preceding line by letters such as *yod, resh,* and *dalet.*

FIGURE 142: Spacing letters with verticals

As in all compositions, what is left out—or the negative space—is as important as the positive elements of the design. Since all the letters are not of even width, and in order to avoid either crowding or gaps, it is a good idea to keep round letters such as *pe* or *samekh* fairly close but to leave more space between letters with long verticals, such as *vav, he,* and *tav.* The letters need not remain in rows, but can be moved around to create interesting arrangements, taking care that the letter is not destroyed by too much distortion.

When emphasizing lines, remember that Hebrews "hangs" from a horizontal bar. Either thicken the entire letter, or just the horizontals. Emphasizing the verticals is completely untrue to the nature of the characters.

FIGURE 143: *Lamed* and *bet:* the correct horizontal emphases appear at the left of each letter; the distorted versions, stressing the vertical strokes, at right

There is a huge difference between "Q" and "O" in the Roman alphabet; in Hebrew also, what appears to be a minute difference can completely change a letter. With practice comes familiarity. Those letters that cause the most confusion because of their similarities are: *nun-gimel-bet-khaf; tet-mem; dalet-resh; tav-het-he; ayin-tzadi.* Notice that the bottom horizontal line of the *bet* extends behind the vertical, while the *khaf*, though the same as the *bet,* does not have the "tail." *Khaf* is constructed like the *nun,* but with wider horizontals; the *gimel* is narrow like the *nun,* but its base line is set at an angle to the vertical.

The *tet* is open at the top, while the *mem* is open at the bottom. The *dalet* is more angular than the *resh;* its top extends behind the vertical, while the *resh* can be seen as curving slightly into the vertical. The *het* is closed at the top; *he* is open; and the *tav* has a little "foot." The *tzadi* is more angular than the *ayin*.

The first *alef-bet* shows the basic structure of each unadorned letter. Many variations of these skeletal forms are possible, but the basic structure must be kept in mind.

FIGURE 144: Basic structure of the *alef-bet*

CROSS STITCH ALEF-BETS

These cross stitch *alef-bets* were all based on ten stitches to the inch, because that is the gauge mesh of the most commonly used needlepoint canvas, and cross stitch canvas usually comes in this mesh as well. The crosses can be easily enlarged or reduced. The other *alef-bets* can also be worked in cross stitch by first drawing them onto a piece of graph paper and then filling in the shapes with the appropriate number of stitches. These are probably the simplest to fit into the grid pattern of canvas work unless much smaller-gauge canvas is used. The letters are shown without their final forms which are simple to work out when you need them.

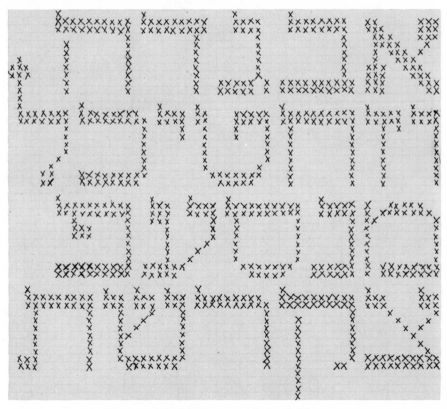

FIGURE 145: Small cross stitch *alef-bet*

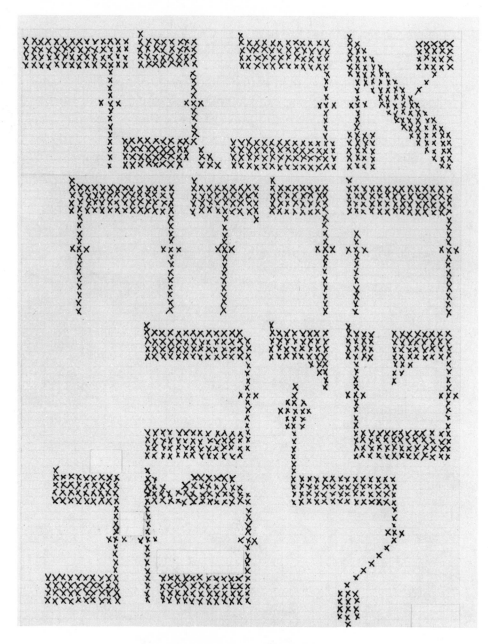

FIGURE 146: Large cross stitch *alef-bet*

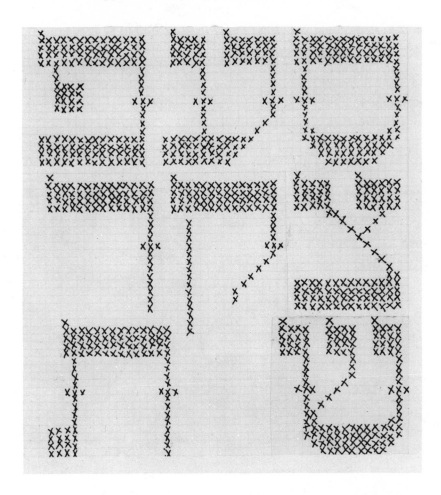

CRENELLATED LETTERING

These letters are based on inscriptions painted on the wall
of King David's tomb on Mount Zion in Jerusalem. The crenellations, domes, and crowns are suggestive of this ancient city
and of royalty. This style of lettering is most appropriate for
the names of kings and queens, for names and words connoting
royalty, and for phrases and quotations relating to Jerusalem.

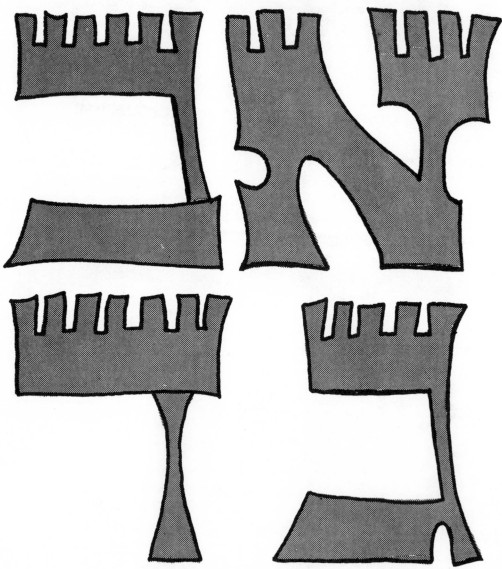

FIGURE 147: Crenellated lettering

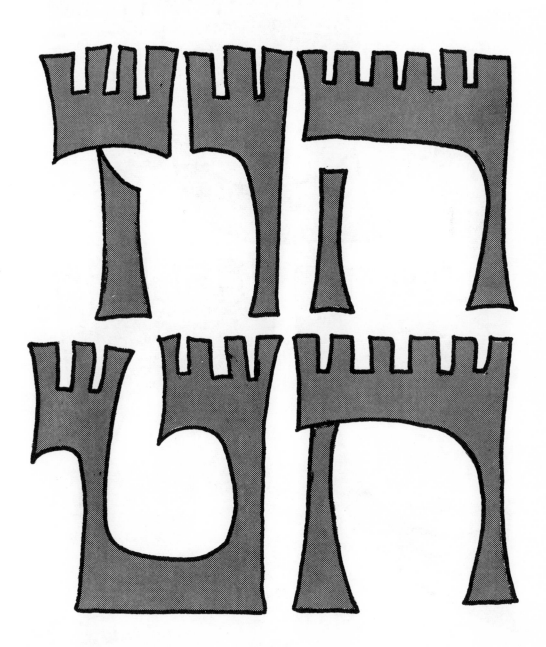

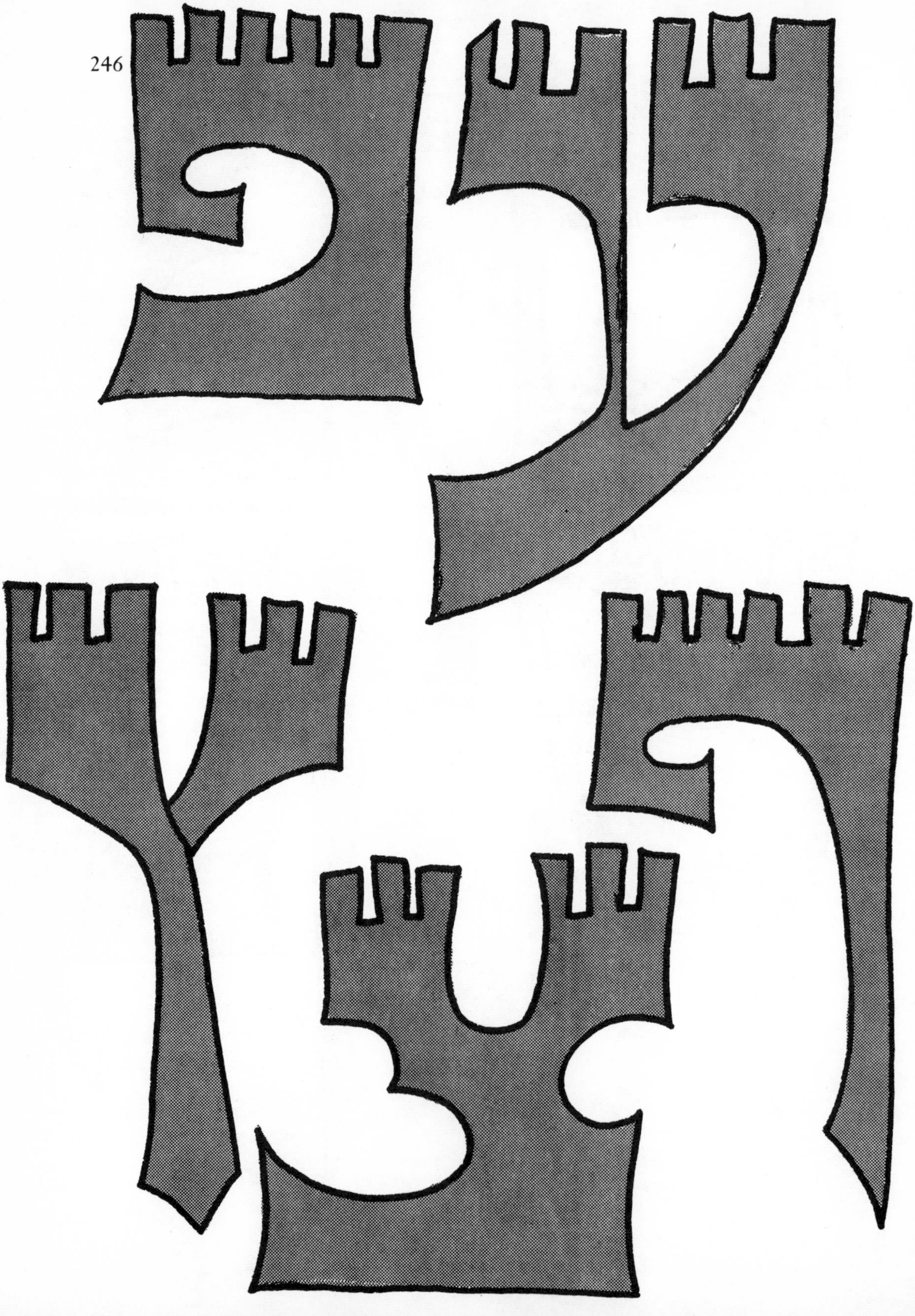

MODERN ALEF-BET

This *alef-bet* is based on the style of lettering called
"Yerushalmi." Although the letters appear modern, their shapes
are derived from the letters engraved on ancient stones in
Jerusalem. Ben Shahn has created a beautiful and—from the
point of view of embroidery—a very useful contemporary
alef-bet. It appears in narrative form in a slender volume en-
titled *The Alphabet of Creation* (New York: Schocken Books,
1965).

FIGURE 148: Modern *alef-bet*

TRADITIONAL ALEF-BETS

You will find this traditionally styled *alef-bet* (I've also included a variation of it) to be useful for different embroidery projects. When filled with different stitches, it takes on the appearance of "illuminated" lettering.*

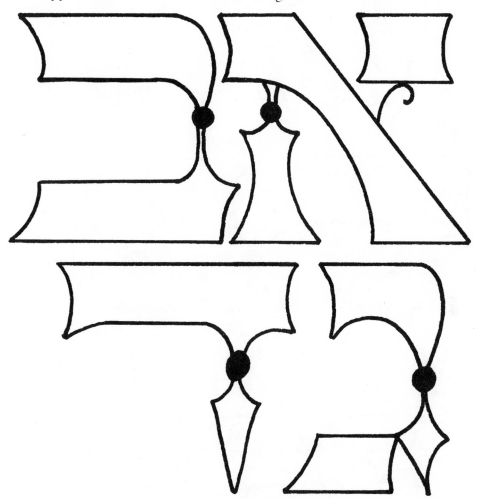

FIGURE 149: Traditional *alef-bet*

*An excellent sourcebook for those interested in further study of the *alef-bet* is *The Art of Hebrew Lettering* by L. F. Toby (Tel Aviv, 1970). It is a small book not generally available in libraries but could be ordered through a Jewish bookstore.

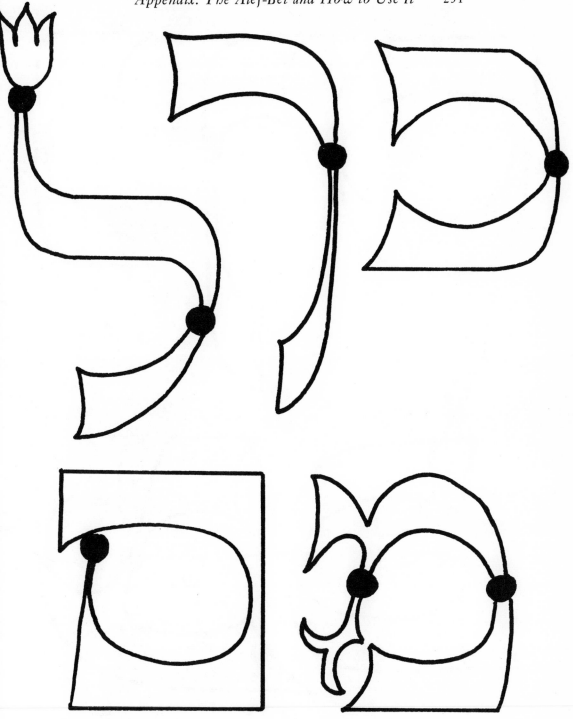

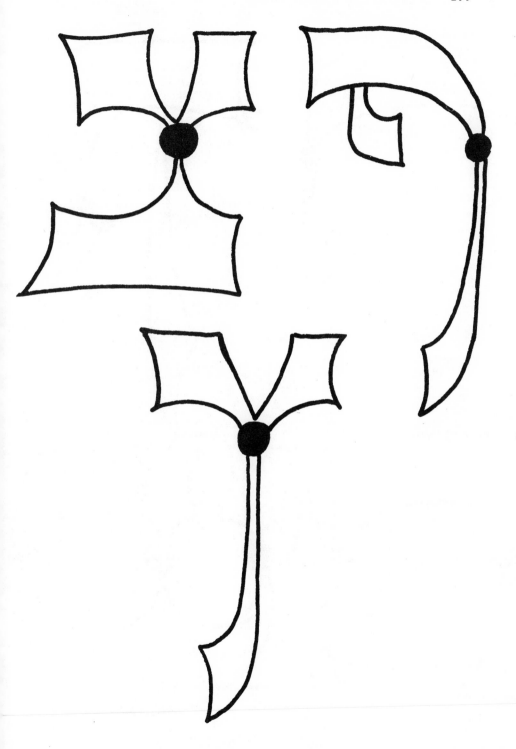

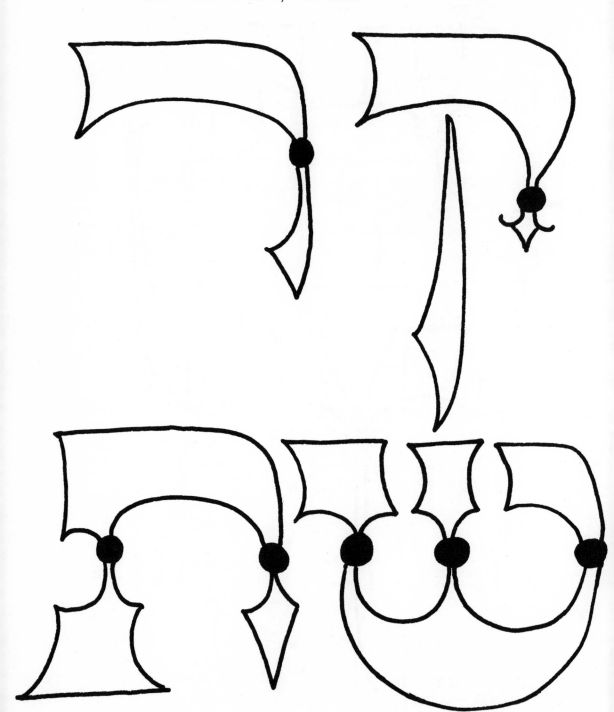

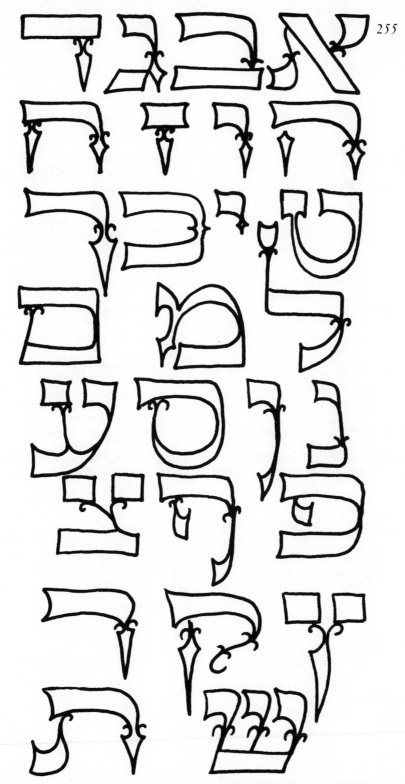

FIGURE 150: Variation on the traditional *alef-bet*

Index

Numbers in italics refer to the illustrations.